T0196399

Eternal Connection

Eternal Connection

Dimensional Word Selection

Daniel Feindt

authorHOUSE®

AuthorHouse™ LLC
1663 Liberty Drive
Bloomington, IN 47403
www.authorhouse.com
Phone: 1-800-839-8640

Published by AuthorHouse   10/03/2013

ISBN: 978-1-4918-2366-8 (sc)
ISBN: 978-1-4918-2367-5 (e)

Library of Congress Control Number: 2013918019

To all the travelers on life's journey,
Moving with grace through eternity,
As the inner compass navigates,
The present moment destiny waits.

Preface

There is a gentle kindness that life shows at times, & being able to write this book is a sign of that design. With anything that is stable & strong, a good foundation needs to be built. To honor the precious structure that life is, I try my best to show gratitude & thanks for those things in life that are a miracle for me.

I find importance in believing that good things happen & there is a power much greater than anything I currently know. This Divine Intelligence guides, protects, loves, shows grace, & exhibits compassion. I pray this is given to all of the loved ones in my life, in which you are one.

I want to visualize & imagine; I want to write to embrace this moment, in hopes to bring miraculous experiences into life; for it surrounds us, & is within us. It is within wise action & silence that can prevent the struggles in life. When I let go & allow life to take me by the hand & lead me down a new path, it is a future unfolding towards an extraordinary perspective.

In 1999, I was diagnosed as schizophrenic by medical professionals, who had found my behavioral actions in day to day life were hurting me rather than helping me. During one of the lowest parts of my life, I started writing poetry as a way to sort out thoughts & express my emotions. In my struggles, I was burning bridges left & right, losing long time friendships, & feeling very lost in the world. My writing was what helped me keep my sanity intact as much as was possible at the time. The first piece of literature I wrote & assembled was a nine chapter book entitled, "Poetic Perception: Through the Eye of the Beholder"

As the years went on I began to regain focus & clarity. I began to observe my personal philosophy, how thought had an effect on my life, & the spiritual principles that really made sense to me. I assembled pocket size books of 40 poems in each paperback. The book you are reading now, comprises of six sections of poetry. Each section was originally one of the pocket size books I had put together throughout the years. With any kind of research as to the writing I have done in the past, you will find a scattered list of what I've put online.

This book is a compilation of 240 poems in total. You may notice the style of writing slightly changing throughout the course of the book. The subject matter also changes as I went through experiences & wanted to document them in poem form. These poems are an effort to explain what I have learned that has truly helped me to regain & maintain stability. My vision is to reach out to anyone who can relate to what I have written, they will be encouraged & helped by knowing they are not alone in life's challenges. The loneliness I have felt has been alleviated by other artist's expression, in writing, music, or movies. So I find no reason why this book wouldn't be a source of comfort to others as well.

Thank you for your interest in reading this book & taking your time to experience what I have to share. I hope this book will be as beneficial for you to read as it was for me to write.

Table of Contents

DIVINE ENERGY

(A Collection of Spiritual Poetry)

Our Journey

I pray the angels watch over you,
For your desires & wishes to come true,
How we think the way a situation is,
God created our lives, this world, all that is,
A possible view from what you know,
It may affect the way things will go,
I believe He wants good things for us,
With a knowing, with faith, & with trust,
Each of us traveling toward what will be,
Staying tuned in to the divine energy,
The Holy Spirit within us will reside,
As the Good Sheppard will guide,
These things, these people, this place,
We travel our journey through time & space.

Calm Energy

I would like to send a universal vibe,
A calm energy within your inside,
A smooth pulse surrounding this place,
God's divine plan, God's peaceful grace,
A unified thought, a harmonious emotion,
A strong foundation, a moment in motion,
This opportunity to express my devotion,
My appreciation of life for instance,
To write a poem was only a notion,
Honoring the creation of my existence,
To share with others my knowing,
With God's love that meets my need,
God's forgiveness is always showing,
Time moves forward, as it will proceed.

Divine Theory

There is no time like the present,
A worldwide moment, that God has sent,
The sight & sound found in this place,
Simple joys & a smile on your face,
Now we are alive; we have these dreams,
The beginning may not be what it seems,
Human intellect with a divine theory,
Writing this so it will be given to me,
Sincerely wanting the best for you,
Only if the intentions are true,
A stone thrown in a still pond,
Similar to the waves of sound,
The ripples of water will spread,
Our voice & words, only once said.

This Moment

Letting go of what is most important,
To be amazed at how it will return,
No way to be late for this appointment,
Only the blessing of what I will learn,
The opportunity to give away this moment,
For the treasure of what is next,
A river's stream of forward movement,
Of what is all simply complex,
When you look for a situation to arrive,
There will always be another chance to try,
Gliding smoothly toward your destination,
Viewing the horizon of what will happen,
As time moves forward with no hesitation,
To enjoy this moment we are in.

Every Heart Beat

If we honor our Creator on just one day,
Limiting the thanks to only a Sunday,
For every heart beat is a new creation,
Every moment is a new situation,
Every breath is an opportunity to express,
The miracles in which I am impressed,
Living a life that God continues to share,
Choosing how to view what has been made,
If I don't realize how much God cares,
I'm concerned my hope may fade,
The soul within my self has grown,
Going through what we've gone through,
Observing what I have already known,
The concept of now is always new.

Apprehension

All we have is the present moment,
Yet I question if we truly own it,
Why do I choose this pause of action?
It must be beyond my comprehension,
Will it delay certain satisfaction?
Holding back with my apprehension,
Will you understand my silence?
Will you know that I care?
I am only fumbling through these events,
Without you I am not there,
With you I am still here,
To think what is now was once then,
To be whispered in your ear,
To be written down with a pen.

Sorry

When another person is involved,
Times I've wanted to do what I shouldn't,
Going back for a problem to be solved,
To make it right, but I couldn't,
Within ourselves, or given from others,
Sisters, brothers, friends, or lovers,
A word or action leading to someone's tears,
Whether it's someone we just met,
Or someone we've known for years,
A simple confusion is what we will get,
So I'll pray to ask for guidance,
My intention was not meant to be untrue,
To break this shallow silence,
To say sorry means, "I Love You".

My Inner Being

From the old to the new school,
With paper and ink as a tool,
The thought being the treasure,
Something incapable of being measured,
The thought being my inner being,
This being is beyond thinking and seeing,
To travel somewhere new or different,
My inner being is the only thing permanent,
It is the spirit throughout the living,
Abundantly taking and giving,
As the material in my world manifests,
My inner being rests,
This is my home,
Taking it with me where I roam.

Dreaming

Waking up, eyes half open,
Seconds to minutes, time gone by hoping,
Expression of inner belief,
Let go to find some relief,
Certain things left as they are,
Only a thought or action away,
Closing the distance, near and far,
Repeated as it is remembered in what I say,
Is it time to meet again or to say goodbye?
Unless I can see you as I sleep,
Once said and done, to give this a try,
A risk taken with faith and a leap,
Open dictionary, words, and meanings,
Moving through what I must be dreaming.

Possibilities

Looking with perspective to now see,
Possibilities of what could be,
Offers to hold out a hand to you,
Only given with what's sincere and true,
With the sky blue & what's discovered new,
This grew continually straight through,
Eyes begin to open to see the time is night,
Light refracting to give these eyes sight,
A vision of what was done is right,
To know our embrace held each other tight,
What is now will soon be what was then,
Decisions of what, where, why, & when,
These things are wrapped up in a prayer,
That uncovers why they were always there.

My Voice

I choose my life to be,
With a divine plan guiding me,
If I choose to fall from dharma,
By anger, hatred, or bad karma,
Then each good deed is a step,
To reach the mountain top of enlightenment,
A brand new view, different than before,
Everything I could want, nothing more,
Except to continue on my path,
Mysteries to solve, truths to grasp,
Music for my soul's satisfaction,
The purpose of my choice,
My actions; my reactions,
My silence; my voice.

Needing the Other

One, two, three,
Variety in society,
Drop of water from the sea,
That has been in you and me,
Recycled throughout the world,
The flat earth becomes curled,
Ashes to ashes, dust to dust,
Finite and infinite are a must,
Each needing the other,
Related as a sister to a brother,
The sun to the moon,
Midnight moving towards noon,
Time and space,
Everything is in its place.

Meditation & Thought

How do I get to know you by what's inside?
I speak without saying the feelings I hide,
Giving me time to think what to do,
Illustrating action,
Mostly meditation,
Thought through,
I could wait for things to change,
A passive approach; reverses to rearrange,
I'm sitting here unknowing,
Not moving or growing,
I think about what patience can bring,
Winter time thoughts wait for the spring,
I'll hold on, hold tight,
I can recognize hope within sight.

A Point of View

A conversation of unspoken word,
Listen to the music unheard,
Timeless echo I hear,
Clouded skies now clear,
A situation the heart evades,
A phrase to a word that fades,
In your eyes the absence of time,
Inspiring a poetic rhyme,
The thoughts placed in your hand,
Flowing through the shifting sand,
Come forward toward the within,
Where you're going; where you've been,
Transcend to me a point of view,
Of what is similar within me & you.

Don't Worry

Time and distance wouldn't keep us apart,
The beginning to end, the end to a new start,
There's a feeling I don't know what's next,
Although I feel I'm going to be okay,
Accepting of not knowing,
The questions perplexed,
So I can move onto the rest of the day,
Moving toward a life surrendered,
By the way things have been rendered,
I'm always going to be human,
Because of my emotions,
And how I go through them,
It will all work out for the best somehow,
So relax, sit back and don't worry for now.

A Thought Away

All connected in some way,
Always has been, even today,
You're a thought away,
Do you agree with what I say?
Soon it will be a new year,
Something I shouldn't fear,
Because of God's love,
An abundance meeting my needs,
Looking at the sky above,
Trusting how it proceeds,
A network of what's true,
Expanding out to you,
The beauty of this place,
All moves with God's grace.

I'll Know What to Say

Knowing you're doing the right thing,
May limit the possibilities that life brings,
But the feeling inside the soul,
Will get me through the time to pay the toll,
The impact on the world around me,
Leads to the closeness of friends and family,
And the innocence inside of me,
Like a child, Christmas morning by the tree,
Any day that I need to face the fear,
Of temptations around me, closer than near,
Hopefully I remember to pray,
To think of heaven in some way,
And if I enter there, on that day,
I'll know what to say.

Portrait of a Family Tree

A family together,
Working to help each other,
Realizing the preciousness of each moment,
Solving while we're evolving,
The chances we all encounter,
To follow love and walk together,
Taking each step as an opportunity,
Connecting in the parallels we all share,
As the leaves of a tree soak up the sunlight,
We shall soak up the water of knowledge,
So young ones can be supported,
Knowing that by working together,
All obstacles can be overcome,
We can pave the way to a brighter day.

Beautiful Memory

The days went fast,
The time went slow,
It felt like it was going to last,
The future led us where we would go,
We talked about God,
We talked about times missed,
She'd agree as she'd nod,
And then one day we kissed,
Was it the beginning of the end?
The end of the beginnings,
It was a vibe I wanted to send,
Why was I worried about sinning?
As things developed and things changed,
I was guided with feelings widely ranged.

God Above

If I were to try and describe,
The love that's by my side,
Of emotions felt in the internal,
That of the surrounding external,
A moving flow,
A quiet stillness we want to know,
This is to be interlaced in our destiny,
Diplomatic immunity beyond what we see,
With infinite knowledge and wisdom,
The infinite time of God's kingdom,
The one with you when you die,
The one who made the ever changing sky,
To summarize God is to say love,
This is how I would describe God above.

The Direction of Time

Walking down a path,
Knowing I can never turn back,
Despite the direction that I go,
Time takes me further, this I know,
Yet, what am I heading toward?
There is always an opportunity,
There is always a possibility,
There is always a hope,
There are always tears to cope,
Or words to express,
That trust in faith leads to happiness,
To move forward in time,
Focused eyes, straight ahead to see,
There is a relationship between you & me.

Still with Me

As the words come around,
Where the sky meets the ground,
My thoughts move elsewhere,
It's probably not rare,
But there are others,
Sisters and brothers,
Just missing her voice,
But I have a choice,
To believe she's still with me,
Choice, fate, or destiny,
The words that she's said,
They are now in my head,
The spirit that connects,
Something I should respect.

Romantic Love

In my heart & in my mind,
In the people I find,
I can visualize your face,
I can hear your voice,
As soft as satin and lace,
You will always be my choice,
It could be that every woman I've known,
Has manifested into what you've shown,
Transcending into love,
Surrounding, below, within, & above,
As it surrounds and flows through,
Constantly changing, always new,
Thank you for this time to write to you,
Amazing how quickly a relationship grew.

Guided by Wisdom

Can there be a right or a wrong decision?
If guided by God's wisdom,
I just want to be me,
Enjoying life in the things I see,
This beginning is in the middle,
Is this something big or little?
When there is something to talk about,
It is in the air as a whisper, not a shout,
Listening for truth is a choice,
This is only my view & my voice,
At times, I worry; what I'm missing?
Yet, to do right, is what I'm wishing,
The varying decisions I make,
There are calculated risks in life to take.

Change My Life

Should I get into my emotions?
To think about past times,
Maybe I'll just go through the motions,
And ignore the traffic signs,
Chew some gum, blow a bubble,
Behave myself, then, get into trouble,
All that is possible; can it be done?
The things I can't change,
Being hurt; being on the run,
Maybe someone could rearrange,
To guide me & keep me in line,
To inspire for the rest of my life time,
One thing will lead to the next thing,
All the happiness it will bring.

The Spirit Within

There are many things of this dimension,
To imagine it might bring some attention,
With a spirit that stays within,
I relax & try my best not to sin,
It would be wise to test the spirit,
To go from there,
As to tell if it is holy,
To know its home is from where,
As the Holy Spirit resides,
It helps take care of the ones I love,
It's been rumored this is a phenomenon,
Taking the form of a dove,
Or in the city it could be a pigeon,
This may help with your decision.

Learning about Myself

I met her when I was twenty,
A good vibe & the love was plenty,
We helped each other to figure out our lives,
Sincere conversation to avoid lies,
We would walk & hold hands,
We talked about foreign lands,
We discussed what we should do,
Because of what we went through,
Good times, tough times, confusing times,
Trying to get over my time of crimes,
Something difficult to describe,
Things I want to hide,
Maybe I thought it was personal,
Yet it feels good to remember her.

What to Do Now

Soft breeze in my face,
Trees emotional from losing their leaves,
Falling at a steady pace,
No more flowers, no more bees,
Cold & bare, you weren't there,
But I was & I was alone,
Confused in knowing that you care,
Something I should have known,
Frost & snow, ice & all that you know,
A black crow, speaking his mind,
The time when new life doesn't grow,
Wound up tight, time to unwind,
Express yourself in words & actions,
It is thought through with slow reaction.

The Wonderful Things

A question arrives of this matter,
How to be thankful,
While still looking for more to do,
A Creator within infinite possibility is how,
No ending to the good things of now,
Why do some have more & others less?
Why does struggle only lead to more stress?
A choice to tune into our Source,
To take in the Holy Spirit of course,
To give my problems to a higher power,
Telling God that I need some help with this,
Knowing that soon there will be an hour,
That I will overcome,
As I enjoy my happiness.

Universal Law

To view a perspective spiritually,
Or to look within with psychology,
My focus on what I would like to see,
Is what will arrive to me,
Thinking about something long enough,
With positive thoughts guided carefully,
Choosing to follow the easy path,
As I avoid the rough,
For as we think, so we shall be,
Is this what Universal Law is about?
The present moment is the cup,
From which I must drink,
Right now & from here on out,
To live my life how I think.

Trying to Describe Heaven

Could it be heaven I'm looking for?
A place of love in the purest form,
Wondering what will happen,
When I knock on the door,
Will it be standard life or far from the norm?
It might be a resting place,
Peace for the one's with pain,
A soul moving gracefully,
Instead of a body with a brain,
Obviously I'm not there yet,
So I'll live my life right,
So I won't have regret,
Thinking about the time we met,
I wonder what hasn't happened yet.

The Distance between Us

How could I have thought to blend it in?
I don't know where this will end,
I'm not sure if a change will begin,
Yet I know I can call her a friend,
These thoughts are inconsistent,
Difficulty of patience & persistence,
Confusing lack of focus remains intact,
But I'm pretty sure I have time to react,
The voice telling me to not stay home,
So I'll leave in an attempt to not be alone,
Natural laws in motion to keep me in line,
Words spoken through the grape vine,
A perspective of your true character,
You're an actress, & I'm an actor.

Balance

Could there be a balance?
Persistence & patience,
Could there be a balance?
Needing others & having self-reliance,
Thoughts to remain in harmony,
A time alone needing to just be,
A time to share kindness in words or action,
With others, to complete a satisfaction,
Learning to know our self, day by day,
Hopefully radiating towards others in a way,
To wait for our desires to arrive,
Yet moving forward,
Step by step,
Stride by stride.

Choices

Uh oh, I made another decision,
It was something I had to do,
Can I take it back & make a revision?
Maybe with the next choice I choose,
Was it the best thing for me?
Was it the best thing for you?
It seems like they're branches on a tree,
They're connected the whole way through,
Regardless of the definition,
Of what it does or what it is,
Choices are part of a long expedition,
It'd be good to know how to pass its quiz,
I should make a choice to make a choice,
It's the way actions can have their voice.

In My Heart & Mind

To walk through life & go to a place where,
I'll cross my fingers & say a prayer,
To leave a place comfortable only to find,
It's still there in my heart & in my mind,
I think about the first time I thought,
How can my dreams be caught?
If I listen & look around,
A potential within something new found,
What I write tonight will be brief,
To sort things out & find some relief,
This could be something to share,
To the people I've mentioned,
It's important for me to show some care,
A purpose speaks, to seek prevention.

One through Ten

Right now I'm wondering who you are,
The person who will stand out from the rest,
I will have to travel from near to far,
Working rather than rest; puts me to the test,
Grace through others, so that I can see,
Peeking through time, space, & infinity,
It's when this will begin to make sense,
Struggles conquered; I need no defense,
Keeping busy, to get this off my mind,
While busy it surfaces a different kind,
Where you are, this message will go,
To you, a person who knows,
One step at a time is the way it goes,
One through ten is the way that it grows.

We Both Cared

To know what was shared in a stare,
Is to know that we both cared,
You could travel for a new place to dwell,
It could be much better, only you can tell,
What I'd like to tell you in these rhymes,
A journey within, mind, space, & time,
Thoughts to travel within while here,
Something new; neither far or near,
In this world of concern,
Money & wellbeing is learned,
I'd like to think there's something better,
As the world is turned,
It could be the love of family & friends,
A mystery is the beginning after this ends.

The Mystery of People

The world surrounds me,
The people are out and about,
What they're about is a mystery,
Time moving forward without a doubt,
Interaction with words & expression,
Anywhere from ecstatic to depression,
Emotions felt; I look back with memories,
Focusing forward, directed like a breeze,
Poetic verses of life to share with you,
What I went through, some courage grew,
Giving back what's been given,
Would that leave me at being even?
With wit and emotion,
It's just a notion when lives are in motion.

The Temple of My Heart

The temple of my heart,
Built from the end to the start,
Synchronistic divine intervention,
As you read what I mention,
I will not believe the heart is limited,
For me, that is a lack of faith,
Courage to not be intimidated,
In the temple of my heart, I am safe,
I hope to always feel this love,
Created by God above,
I need to maintain this strength,
Faith protecting inside & out,
From a small distance to a great length,
As I try to share what this is about.

Giving Thanks

How can a bee be thankful?
The pollen the flowers give,
How can a writer be thankful?
The ideas they've been given,
How can wisdom & knowledge be shared?
Without asking questions,
How can a musician or dancer be thankful?
The rhythms of life,
How can an actor or actress be thankful?
The varieties of character,
How can I be thankful?
You are a part of my life.

MOMENT IN MOTION

(Expression of Poetic Progression)

Where I Am Now

A moment in time; I picked up this book,
It is now a memory; I can take a look,
What will happen turning this page?
If you count the hours, what is your age?
Can you visualize what will happen next?
Will you decide to read the rest of this text?
We are in the now; a constant blessing,
A constant change is awake while resting,
I feel that it is a beautiful thing,
What will this moment continue to bring?
I'll choose how the moments will go,
Because of what I believe & know,
Enjoy this time; play with reality,
This moment moves with immortality.

Allowing to Unfold

I'll look away to allow the possibilities,
For possibility is merely synchronicity,
I cannot see the plan with my human eyes,
A knot my assumption ties,
I shouldn't stare at the sun,
To be blinded by what is already done,
Although in my life it is the light,
The vibe sometimes is intensely bright,
So I turn away & look around me,
A way to tune into something I can see,
My friend, for now I must let you go,
To learn about who I am, I must know,
To keep things simple, thinking clearly,
I want the best to happen so dearly.

A Wish

A wish to find; a wish granted,
Possibilities of a seed planted,
A wish for when the time is right,
Natural progression from day to night,
Expanding out this continued emotion,
From a drop of rain, to the ocean,
An indescribable amount of inspiration,
God has perfected all creation,
Waves of thought, each blink of an eye,
Amazing to comprehend; I don't ask why,
We've established a genuine trust,
Because we want to, not because we must,
Do all wishes come true?
I feel if only it is what it's intended to do.

Relationship Alignment

The time has moved forward,
A beautiful shift in words,
A mysterious change in vibe,
The perspectives will finally combine,
Words & actions may indicate,
The world is in a perfect state,
Manifesting in experiences,
A knowing of how real this is,
Although the intensity, I feel relaxed,
Truth of love, with emotional facts,
What will be is right now,
I won't have to worry how,
What will be is a union,
An alignment together is within.

Anticipation

Looking forward to what will arrive,
Currently feeling the excitement inside,
Only wanting the best for you,
I hope you know that is true,
The respect I have for your choice,
This opportunity for you to hear my voice,
Yet you should know that when I pray,
It is a request for you to stay,
Wanting to honor your freedom,
Smiling at the memories as I see them,
Wanting for you to live and enjoy,
You've captured the heart of this boy,
The innocence and romance will blend,
I wish only the best for you my friend.

A Magnetic Pull

I feel I'm being led to act,
In what way will others react?
Take the chance to follow this force,
Truly hoping there will be no remorse,
Only being pulled in a natural direction,
To do no wrong is my selection,
Two magnets faced in the right direction,
Hold tight with amazing precision,
I don't want to turn them around,
An opposing barrier will surround,
Needing patience to make these decisions,
Once an action is taken, is there revision?
Hoping for the divine wisdom to guide,
I hope only to relax and enjoy the ride.

Synchronize & Align

Realizing I'm not alone in all this,
You have comforted; I have felt bliss,
Yet limited to individual perspective,
A person's eye sight is subjective,
Should I try to apply concepts?
To my life & to this world,
Attaching a thought to this moment,
Now in the past, no way to own it,
A synchronized or aligned action,
With each person something is matching,
Temporarily disconnecting a view,
Yet with what I see, I think it's true,
The blessing of an offbeat movement,
In a way this continues through it.

Illuminated Presence

To say what is already known,
There is a light in you, now grown,
Those you have illuminated with presence,
Something very unique within your essence,
You've learned so much and come so far,
A love expanding as a light, as a star,
The reason I haven't lost my way,
Close and caring in the thoughts you say,
You have been with me; a guide, a friend,
Inspiration to write with a pen,
Encouragement during times of sadness,
Showing kindness in that, & hope in this,
A thought to a word, a word to an action,
I'll honor who you are in reaction.

Honoring Love

Love takes no form,
As it expands from within,
Like clothing once worn,
Now a different outfit I'm in,
My sleep leads to being awake,
I'll breathe in, then, breathe out,
Exchanging the air I give & take,
What the un-manifested will bring about,
Does life have a recipe?
In which the ingredients I choose,
Perspectives of you & me,
Giving a gift of nothing to lose,
To shine a light; to see a new view,
A mystery reveals an experience of clues.

A Pure Beauty

It couldn't have happened any other way,
Memories we share will lead me to pray,
To continue the brilliance of an opportunity,
The hope of things soon to be,
I will live for her soft smile,
To think of her as I walk each mile,
I will live for the gaze of her eyes,
Something I could never deny,
Her beauty in physical form,
Since the day she was born,
It radiates the vibe of her inner being,
A true essence is the meaning,
Privileged in the time we've spent together,
Perspective of connection is forever.

Calming the Mind

The stimulus of thought within an idea,
Will I project it with emotional energy?
Unfold the action to be,
A way to experience what we see,
If exploration of the mind is documented,
In this way grace will be presented,
Applying this to the current situation,
A day dreamer rarely needs vacation,
Fascinated with this time concept,
If after the next is before the next,
Don't worry; I'm only continuing,
An idea increasing will soon be dwindling,
A calm mind is a blessed thing,
In my pocket is what I'll bring.

Emotional Response

I'll listen to a music instrumental,
Trying to apply to the spiritually mental,
Listening to music with no lyrics,
Performed with guitar strings & picks,
It leads me to non-directed thought,
Projecting a sound wave now caught,
Enjoying the speed of beat and rhythm,
The pace of the thought pattern,
It approaches an adjusting time frame,
This is absolutely not the same,
The vibe of the music has entered within,
Is now a good time to confess a sin?
The emotional response of the stimulus,
Repeating this makes it continuous.

Being Alive Now

A good time for this moment,
All around of what is currently present,
An epiphany of being alive now,
I don't feel the need to ask how,
Yet, a wonderful choice of view,
Updating with others what is new,
The progression into the future,
Movement to the next is for sure,
I may say less and express more,
Finding peace with the memories I store,
A calm outlook of what this is,
The merging of her; the merging of his,
In what this situation is about,
Guidance towards no doubt is the best route.

Enjoying the Moment

Will my concerns take away from today?
Will I worry how others view what I say?
Do my actions and words have an effect?
Will it be wrong or will it be correct?
An interesting concept to think of control,
A focus to take the weight off my soul,
This is out of my hands, I have to admit,
I know a solution as I write where I sit,
Reminded of the point of living this day,
To enjoy this moment in some way,
Things will come and go this hour,
The best of what is within my power,
I can turn my day around and know,
Life will run a course in what it will show.

Phase Shift

Is life a series of phase shifts?
Will I accept this is what it is?
Once again I'm calm and balanced,
A soft spiritual side can mix with science,
Knowing the time for words or silence,
Friends and family create an alliance,
Where will these thoughts go?
This is something I can only know,
I'm focused on what I'm focused on,
It is from here on to here on,
The eternal realms of love are around,
A moment within the speed of sound,
The physical world of confusion will cease,
It intermingles with the non-physical peace.

The Molecular Soul

I would like to share with you,
An idea that you may find true,
The universe is constantly interacting,
A spiritual source that is always new,
The world, the body, all you can think,
A flowing soul, like the water we drink,
Integrated in time and space,
Interacting without a trace,
The things that can't be explained,
The mind is more than just the brain,
Our view of emotional perspective,
The individuality of the collective,
Feel the soul, feel the spirit,
Find the molecular dance within it.

Underlying Reality

When pure energy is involved,
Deep levels of consciousness,
A part of the mystery is solved,
Networked into forms of intelligence,
These objects hiding an inward disguise,
The most basic thing that exists,
Becoming smaller, decreasing in size,
The unit of energy eternally persists,
This energy takes form as it translates,
Expanding to reveal its outward disguise,
The coming together of things initiates,
Becoming larger, increasing in size,
From atoms, to molecules, to our body,
It continues out from Earth into the galaxy.

Seasons of Transition

A little of that, a little of this,
Moments of struggle, moments of bliss,
What I feel now may be different tomorrow,
A thought can transition to sorrow,
Within life experience, the seasons change,
A constant cycle, moves to arrange,
The circle of life we live,
We must take, we must give,
There will always be growth here,
There is no reason to fear,
Life will happen as time moves through,
We experience life, that much is true,
Fall to winter, winter to spring,
We will make it through what life will bring.

Source of Thought

Am I experimenting with words?
The consciousness of the natural birds,
A previous source of thought is progressing,
Do I care if this is even impressing?
To strike a note; to strike a chord,
I'll just push buttons on a keyboard,
A sound vibration may have been found,
Movements from the scale of sound,
Now from present moment consciousness,
This situation is completely ridiculous,
These words are from previous notes,
They are merely the thoughts I wrote,
Words I attempt to say honestly,
This is a thought pattern written previously.

From My Soul

I open my heart and offer these words,
Writing from my soul; the way I prefer,
To love a woman is a wonderful thing,
All I can give is what I will bring,
Another beginning after this is done,
To find my friend, my special someone,
Have I met her or have we yet to meet?
Nothing more cherished or sweet,
A growing relationship is the creation,
Because it is love that is the situation,
There is nothing more important to me,
It is the definition of my life to be,
All of this happens for a reason,
For my struggle will soon be leaving.

The Next Moment

The unknown next moment,
Centralized within the zone of it,
The erratic movement of energy,
To be rearranged for what could be,
To think of chaotic organization,
A shifting moment of this situation,
For the form of experience to change,
The spectrum of light in infinite range,
To eat & drink of this moment's nutrition,
Self-medicating with optimism,
A safe & secure guided concept,
Physical & spiritual sown within it,
I don't know what's coming up next,
Carefully I'll approach the next moment.

Mentality of Spirituality

Invisible thoughts crafted into this,
Microscopes show the movement of that,
The way a healthy balance can twist,
The religious nature of a cat,
Egyptian style of course,
Relaxing all day, with no remorse,
A trace of communication left,
Documented safely, as to avoid theft,
I feel its God's spiritual energy,
Eternal cycles of what's known as infinity,
Guiding us if we allow & trust,
As it is ashes to ashes; dust to dust,
Constant variables to intrigue & entice,
Individual mergence is oh so nice.

A Vibration Frequency

Whether laws of life or a divine science,
A person's view will decide this,
To think of a vibration frequency,
Emanating from you and me,
To consider an electron being observed,
Although this may seem a little absurd,
It does change what occurred,
What was crystal clear is now blurred,
With quantum physics I can see,
What is to comprehend is a possibility,
Tuning into a desired radio station,
A connection to your destination,
So I don't tune into frustration,
For the frequency of joy is inspiration.

Above the Confusion

I feel it is always a good time,
For the opportunity of a rhyme,
Encourage to rise above the confusion,
A confusing world of illusion,
To be within a passive center point,
Two sides of the same coin,
The middle of a situation can balance,
To me this concept makes sense,
A safe and secure vibe to connect to,
I'll communicate in this way to you,
Feeling what is truly enjoyable,
The easiest and most comfortable,
A citizen of this world with a focus,
Relationships interact in genuine trust.

A Reality Check

Should I maintain this course of thought?
Contemplating the materials I've bought,
Recognizing and affirming a reality check,
An experience in which I'll connect,
What is truly going on in the world?
With a population of people in the plural,
Right now I feel safe and secure,
So it's the confusion I will ignore,
My curiosity wonders if in some way,
Are these thoughts connected to you today?
The present moment of space and time,
Can I help others by attempting a rhyme?
I only want to share what I know,
To encourage within the way this will go.

React to a Fact

Exactly the same; this moment will change,
Compromise the now; a situation arranged,
Truly abstract; observe and interact,
Pick it up, then, put it back,
Looking forward to being alive for a reason,
A memory; a time; a moment; a season,
Things could happen either way,
However, there are the choices of today,
The fine-tuned plan of chaotic movement,
Strategies to move toward improvement,
Some optimism for an emotional baptism,
Focused only upon this brilliant vision,
I know this all makes sense to me,
Yet I hope this is a perspective you can see.

Her Courage

I can only try and describe,
The courage she has inside,
Delicate strength with style and grace,
Moving through the world she must face,
Although the burden may be costly,
She always triumphs softly,
Using her kindness and compassion,
Regardless of knowing the type of reaction,
When the manipulation of others arrives,
With a smile, she always survives,
She listens when I attempt to talk,
Then sadness enters as she begins to walk,
Away from the moment we were together,
I'll pray her love will last forever.

Divine Secrets

The people who know divine secrets,
Maintain its mystery and keep it,
Others will help to pass them on,
Transitioning back from new to known,
For they know this as well,
So the wisdom will selectively tell,
They have brought this enlightenment,
To experience a life of enjoyment,
As we have shown this consciousness,
To balance what is more or less,
This world's contrast of perspective,
Deciding what's best for the selective,
To select what is wanted for the future,
Continuing to align with what's true.

Confidence

There is a situation I am in,
I don't want to wear out my welcome,
How do I know how something will be?
The dream of the future I see,
Choice of perspective in how I want it to be,
It may affect the control I have on destiny,
I will decide to visualize a positive outcome,
Manifesting in the way I want it to become,
Why would I want to over think this?
Instead, I will follow my bliss,
Regardless if I have doubts otherwise,
It will only be a pleasant surprise,
A situation to look forward to,
Confidence will pull me through.

Hope for the Future

I need to do something more than ever,
This journey could last forever,
Dwelling on the past is no way to live,
Realizing I will get what I give,
What do I truly look forward to?
This will help me to know what to do,
Something will sincerely bring me joy,
Using the imagination I had as a boy,
Experiencing the wonder of hope,
I can offer positive thoughts to cope,
Choosing to look to a future of optimism,
To consciously make these decisions.
An attitude of things will get better,
Honoring the friendship I have with her.

Taking a Risk

My attempts at humor,
Seems like taking a risk,
Will it lead to a rumor?
The end of a friendship I will miss,
When should I step back?
To tell myself to hush,
A wise decision I lack,
Or just swept away by a rush,
Do the words bring joy?
Or do they just annoy?
I wonder how much control I have,
My interaction to get attention,
Mistakes or perfection; good or bad,
Trying to be careful with what I mention.

Problems & Solutions

Unfortunately I focused on the problems,
This in no way helped to solve them,
Instead of focusing on the solution,
I continued to allow the pollution,
Spreading the filth of worry,
I couldn't find patience when I hurried,
When I was looking for a better way,
A small voice inside me started to say,
How could I make a change?
What could I shift to finally arrange?
I knew what I had to do & took the action,
It felt right & gave a certain satisfaction,
For once I let go; a new start to begin,
I had found enjoyment of life again.

Optimistic Struggle

Do I know how things really are?
The feelings inside are rather bizarre,
A time when two perspectives interact,
I find I'm unaware how to act,
Wanting things to happen beautifully,
If it doesn't happen, do I take it personally?
Feeling I should have control of this,
Wanting to feel I can make a difference,
Does this limit my vision?
The good intentions in a decision,
It was the best I knew how to do,
The optimistic struggle I'll go through,
Just move with the flow,
Just trust and let go.

Wants & Needs

What do I need? What do I want?
Questions asked; brought to the front,
Back and forth of a changing view,
Vice versa of course; oh, what to do?
I want to have my needs met,
The wants of what hasn't happened yet,
A future time of this traveling moment,
The wants, the needs, do I really own it?
A planned situation, within a conversation,
Gratitude and care for this preparation,
Visualization creates memories known,
The wants & needs of a personality shown,
To be okay, either way,
Do what you do, say what you say.

God's Plan

I believe God has a plan for our lives,
At times I view with divine eyes,
Sometimes I feel asleep during the day,
Do I know what to do or say?
Having faith as our experiences have taught,
Sometimes I feel trapped or caught,
Other times I have the freedom to shine,
Are these things yours or mine?
A concept that we are all a whole,
We are unique despite what we've been told,
The blessings and gifts from God,
We can accomplish what may seem odd,
Realizing God gives us a purpose to know,
We have work to accomplish before we go.

Honoring the Divine

You know my heart; you gave me peace,
Wanting a knowledge that will never cease,
I was lonely, then arrived conversation,
With forgiveness, I cried for the situation,
Feeling sadness; I found a map to happiness,
A return to the eternal home I miss,
Overcoming obstacles through the storm,
The temporary clothes that were worn,
Eyes show vision; the mouth shares words,
A feeling of being alive is now stirred,
Your kindness nurtures as it guides the wise,
You have opened my mind to realize,
I ask for endurance to complete the work,
What you gave and what I took.

Individuality in Unity

We're in this together as one,
Yet the individual spice will spark the fun,
Everybody has a past and a story,
Thinking of the future may bring worry,
We will all find a unity we truly seek,
It's said it will be inherited by the meek,
Each of us is a piece of the infinite,
An ability to add our two cents to it,
Together we can make a selection,
Collected consciousness of an election,
Different ways of looking at the same thing,
With an amazement each view will bring,
We all need a heart to live; we're all unique,
Twenty four hours in each day of the week.

Remember this Time

This is working out to document a time,
When I sit & write rhyme after rhyme,
When I needed to write every day,
To keep afloat and not drift away,
To stand up for my right to live,
Unaware at what these words will give,
To those who choose to read my thoughts,
An expression in the way I was caught,
Feeling pressure of not being good enough,
Doing what I had to when times got rough,
Thoughts continue to run through my head,
I try to keep up & write what they said,
A new beginning; a pleasant change,
As for right now, things are very strange.

A Moment's Creation

Certain thoughts seem to occur,
Will things remain the way they were?
There is a way I'll react to a situation,
Is it part of a moment's creation?
What do I want to apply to this phrase?
Choosing a direct path or a frustrating maze,
An opposite action to remain focused,
Counteract the unwanted I've noticed,
Realize this world and understand,
The way I want to live in this land,
Questioning variables to know the integrity,
It's infinitely away & infinitely toward me,
The source of this origination,
Put this together in a desired configuration.

Complete Trust

As I am sharing these thoughts with you,
I'll offer them with consistent gratitude,
With a complete trust I look forward,
To what God will guide me toward,
Accomplish the things I can do,
A complete faith to see me through,
God will take care of these things for me,
I can't emphasize enough for you to see,
I must let this go and release my requests,
They are now in good hands, so I will rest,
I have handed them over for the blessings,
God will protect the secret I'm confessing,
Possibly the outcome will be in the end,
Better than I could imagine or comprehend.

ETERNITY & TECHNOLOGY

(A Perspective through Poetry)

When Heaven Arrives

A time span on this planet here,
Making the most in a way sincere,
A thought of when Heaven arrives,
Towards the infinite, I close my eyes,
Essence alive in a Spirit complete,
Always a dream, until then we meet,
Beginning to end, the truth in focus,
Blessings in Heaven, a way I'll know this,
For now I will send this home,
My mind will then continue to roam,
Still in love; soaking this into the within,
Beneath the waters of Spirit that I'm in,
To be in love; surrounding my heart,
Now is when this begins to start.

The Person You Knew

Do you remember the person you knew?
I would wait, dedicate, & think of you,
Before we were swept away in situations,
Before I'd chat online with many nations,
The breeze was calm; the sun was out,
It was you that it was all about,
Do I speak with honesty in what I focus?
Varying faith, from a cross to a lotus,
From confusion into clarity of mind,
In this present moment, I feel fine,
I'll try to understand your position in life,
Most likely you'll become someone's wife,
When I needed a friend you were there,
That's why I write this & that's why I care.

The Best Outcome

At this point many are involved,
With an equation to be solved,
There is a way for everyone to arrive,
Integrating what we all want to derive,
The relationship of her and him,
Is now the right time to begin?
Am I to continue the wait?
I'm learning to successfully procrastinate,
I just want to do what's right,
For my dreams to begin to take flight,
I will look for signs to tell,
For this to all work out well,
With you and I, him and her,
It's possible for miracles to occur.

Sincere Surrender

In an authentic way, just letting go,
To be with the essence that life will show,
As to embrace the present moment,
Releasing the idea of a way to own it,
Honestly, I don't know what can happen,
Yet, faith in God's guidance can let it in,
I could be responsible for each thought,
Even the responsibility so early taught,
So much of a surrender to make it happen,
The expectations I may be trapped in,
There is gratitude for what just is,
I know none of these words apply to this,
A knowing in which I'm unable to express,
Humility rewards after failing the test.

Take Flight

I trust I will see you again,
Although I may not know when,
You have taken flight into your world,
Now a woman grown from a little girl,
The dreams embraced as a child,
Within your mind, an imagination so wild,
Now you are exploring these dreams,
I have faith in you, the way it seems,
I'm grateful I have experienced your song,
An interlude; you have waited so long,
Your independence is known & respected,
With the words you said, I was directed,
To know this is what you want here,
Your laughter guided me to what you feel.

Let You Go

I said I would do anything for you,
The most difficult thing to go through,
What if that thing is to let you go?
You'll live your life & I'll never know,
To not be able to share my life with you,
If that is what you want to be true,
If that is what you want me to be,
To wonder why you're away from me,
I'll attempt to do this one thing,
It may leave me lonely in what it brings,
Separation from all I hold dear,
This in fact is my greatest fear,
Is this the reality you want?
In this situation, you are in the front.

The Moments on Earth

As I look back at my time on earth,
Ever since the day of my birth,
I can see this is all going by quickly,
The reason it is precious on this journey,
I know I'm still alive to write this,
I know about the memories I miss,
My growth through an experience,
To arrive here now & probably smile,
Before I leave this body I've known,
There may be much more that's shown,
To think all this has happened so far,
Gives hope of heaven in the stars,
A spiritual bliss because I have lived,
The sweet taste of creation God will give.

Important to Me

One press of a button on a keyboard,
Routed, the designed path, the circuit board,
The electric pulse of the information is zero,
Defined by energy within a wire's interior,
Collect the impulse in temporary memory,
To be calculated in a processor we can't see,
Back out to the random access storage,
Through the modem of a technological age,
A header packet sent to another computer,
I really need to look for a tutor,
To know if all the data is obtained,
Download complete, bandwidth drained,
Enjoy this file, whether mp3 or exe,
For some reason all this is important to me.

Respecting Distance

You have set up the boundaries,
Yet to me this is a mystery,
I will respect the line you have drawn,
Although now I feel like a pawn,
The distance apart you have set,
Inspires questions of why we met,
It takes strength to follow through,
This type of promise to me is new,
Is this a test of my character?
I will respect this, so please tell her,
It was worth it & I'm glad,
In no way do I regret or am I sad,
Only thanks to you, so I'll wonder,
In the richness of life, I will ponder.

A Quiet Sound

Within the surroundings here,
No time to wipe away a tear,
Humbly ask for the Holy Spirit within me,
Given by God, as the air is free,
If a jealousy of life style is near,
Clarifying the thought pattern here,
With no rational reason to fear,
This conformity is entirely too weird,
Flipped around with a quiet sound,
Knowing their observation is around,
Clearing the mentality of confusion there,
An attempt to keep this calm is rare,
To lead to another time of silence,
I'll accept the opportunity to try this.

Until

A form of hope, to travel in this direction,
Delicate & careful in this form of creation,
It will always be missing in life until,
I realize what I look for is here still,
A soft gaze right in front of me,
Is the present moment my destiny?
The choice of how I'll view this day,
A way my inner dialogue chooses to say,
Contentment in an attempt to reply again,
With a phrase I can only write with a pen,
With a thought I can try & convince,
I've overcome every struggle ever since,
I know deep inside what I try to hide,
Life is a ride & in myself I'll confide.

Curiosity

For some reason I feel I need to live,
In a life position where I can give,
There is so much I'm thankful for,
Only God knows what is in store,
Still I don't want to take the chance,
How fragile & graceful is this dance?
A way I will express to you,
What my perspective finds true,
Although I may not think I know,
There is a way this situation will go,
I'm drawn into looking for what to do,
I'm curious if I will interact with you,
Will it lead to the next step?
We can walk in faith to accept.

A Possible Reason

If I can keep the right focus,
To try & encourage all of us,
Temptation may lead me off course,
A possible reason for my remorse,
Choices with good consequence in prayer,
Have I wronged the people who are there?
If everything happens for a reason,
A life allowing an approach of treason,
Open the door to try something new,
Or close one, to end the chapter about you,
I'll remain quiet & careful,
Doing my own thing to be thankful,
We all have individual lives to live,
Individual clarity won't blur what just is.

You Have Arrived

Today is the first day,
It's going to be okay,
Seize the opportunity today,
Can you hear what I'm trying to say?
I want to send out to you love,
With this style & grace from above,
So many people care about you,
You can rise above this to get through,
It may feel like you're barely afloat,
So just visualize yourself in a boat,
Of course there are times that are rough,
The wonderful person you are is enough,
I want you to feel good about who you are,
You have arrived after traveling so far.

Return to the Center

The seconds of a clock, moves with a tick,
Then to a tock, so which one shall I pick?
Or what to do with this time in movement,
Something to live for, no need to prove it,
Return to the center of calm & peace,
An awareness of simplicity to increase,
I may agree I am not my thoughts,
To untie the confusion of mental knots,
Let it go, take a breath,
I will know, what is best,
For you & them, him & her,
The best scenario can occur,
A process of gratitude passes by,
With fun, with thanks, the time flies by.

Quiet & Aware

An available source of information,
What am I looking to apply in this situation?
Realigning my focus to the data obtained,
Or lost in the past story of when it rained,
Now sunny, & I know what I want,
Thoughts; yet which ones are in the front?
Are they based on love or fear?
Trust, faith, & grace, in a life so dear,
Unless impulsive worry & doubt reacts,
Intentionally quiet & aware of how I act,
Consequence in a choice of cause & affect,
To decide if feelings I entertain are correct,
So, realize the miracle & choose wisely,
As I sympathize & understand precisely.

Continue On

The way this will continue on,
Hopefully these words are not my own,
With faith to receive a blessing or gift,
Space time continuum nexus rift,
Opening up possibilities not of me,
Letting go of what I know is my destiny,
Something better than what I could do,
Being parallel to what travels through,
If I arrive at choice & decide,
Neither a decision nor a choice will reside,
Not senseless but rather precious,
Opening up to what is consciousness,
The next step in this walk,
Silence speaks instead of vocalized talk.

Enjoyment of Stability

As much as I'd like to stop,
Submitting to fear with a tear drop,
It's only a matter of deciding,
To take responsibility without hiding,
To keep myself safe within boundaries,
What I share with others around me,
Am I vulnerable to who you are?
I can't actually find any emotional scars,
If I can't touch it, does it exist?
If it doesn't exist, could I persist?
Untangled the words with a twist,
Choosing a choice will need to insist,
Enjoyment of stability for this,
Keeping it simple will lead to a kiss.

A First Impression

For him to speak with his voice,
His mind needed to make a choice,
Of what to say in a phrase,
What he knows from birth until today,
Life lessons, memories, & knowledge,
He met her after he was done with college,
Now needing to offer a first impression,
Will it decide the relationship's progression?
In his mind is the current search for words,
Using language she understands & prefers,
His mouth opens to release a wave of sound,
Within her ear the message sent is found,
With the transfer of the sound received,
His vibe is then pleasantly perceived.

A Mental Code

For some reason it stopped working,
Was it supernatural within lurking?
The screen went blank, a dark black,
Twenty four hours, the power was back,
Meta-physics or wireless networks,
I'll never know why it now works,
Nothing more to say about this,
So I'll listen to music to reminisce,
When the lyrics talk about certain people,
Yesterday I was under a church steeple,
After months I can write another poem,
I wonder if it is caught in the knowing,
So I'll look around, smile, & relax,
A celebration of a mental code cracked.

Where to Focus

Mental images & feelings combine,
When I'm moving toward what I will find,
An awareness of what I'm thinking,
Affecting the mind as if what I am drinking,
The sip of one flavor, to identify it as bad,
Feeling angry is the same as feeling sad,
Be careful when exploring thoughts,
Only a good vibe to what it starts,
If I can recognize what I don't want,
A return to a routine, now in front,
To look back at the unwanted,
Although it was wanted to be confronted,
To now know what I can take,
Applying it to the next experience I'll make.

This is the Time

Know when to let down the act,
Illusions of what isn't a fact,
Hope between what is blurred,
Patterns of light in the darkness occurred,
The tears streamed out of my eyes,
I must put on this outward disguise,
I can't let on that I feel this way,
A fragile glass carried on a silver tray,
Leveraged carefully, moving this thought,
The beverage has now been bought,
This is the time to not give up,
Just take one more sip from the cup,
Life is just that, one at a time,
Just as this is merely a rhyme.

Starting to Pray

Is faith in the unseen the way?
To arrive in Eternal Heaven one day,
To stay true to my heart's desire,
With purity as intense as fire,
To burn away the unwanted thought,
Making ashes of what I am not,
Unfortunately I don't know what to say,
There is hesitation in starting to pray,
So for right now the action I need,
Writing thoughts as I want to proceed,
Although I cannot see outside of time,
I can guide my thoughts with this rhyme,
If I feel there is nowhere to turn,
I'll keep myself safe in what I have learned.

I Once Knew

Only by the grace of God, I am here,
The repetitive nature is becoming clear,
Rearrange the furniture for something new,
A view to run from, that I once knew,
Small movements, I may question direction,
Courageous enjoyment, given in protection,
The memories may still be attached,
Infinite images to try & be matched,
Yet I know with continued faith & hope,
I will use my heart & mind to cope,
Some times with intellect & wisdom,
Not knowing where I've come from,
My past history, & all the moments,
Divine intervention selects this within it.

Digital Molecules

Information collected has been assembled,
The end point; duplicate exactly resembled,
A form of blue print, from here, to go there,
All aspects; object transported with care,
Digital molecules & transportation,
Atomic material & digital information,
Organized & directed by invisible software,
Matter moved with technological hardware,
So that's my imagination's concept,
As direct as I could get it,
Could this device manifest into reality?
Moving things as a grain of salt in the sea,
As a molecular structure floats in air,
The data is wirelessly moved with care.

Into the Air

What sense does it make?
Holding it in & being fake,
What is really on my mind?
Answers to the questions I want to find,
I could hide from just one word,
Maybe that would be absurd,
Truth setting a thought free,
Into the air; into a tree,
Family, friends, & those around me,
With this notion I just want to be,
No worries concerning my care for you,
Or to what I think they go through,
Simply put, the sky is now blue,
So fate can contemplate what to do.

In Some Way

Pull this together & continue on,
You know what you must do,
You may feel your heart was torn,
But once again the sky is blue,
You made it through an event,
You cried your tears as a way to vent,
So now the daily responsibilities are here,
Are they complete, if so, how far or near?
Make a list; I know I can do this,
Get the gist? With a flick of the wrist,
The day is not done yet, more to do,
To care about what happens to you,
Please focus & know this will work out,
In some way, know what this is about.

Traveling to Walk

Symbolizing what is outlined in the past,
Permission for nothing to browse,
Large amounts discovered, not there,
Constructing location to input the outcome,
3 of approximately twenty, necessarily as is,
Rapid pace, change focus to be the same,
Transmission complete, just the surface,
Say one more word, ulterior motives,
You won't see me for a while,
After the night is home now,
Run the block seated in the cement,
Currency of monetary, electricity flowing,
To take the pool & re-locate the H2O,
I'm traveling to walk, for all that you are.

Data Transfer

I could pretend I know what to write,
Passively continue to fight the good fight,
When I don't know where to turn,
I've given up all that I've learned,
Yet today I will go back online,
A keyboard that will never be mine,
To search, discover, express and find,
Communicate & observe to pass the time,
I'll withdraw to the world I know,
Digitally addictive, a part of the show,
Electronic data transfer to her,
Again awake, to the now, in a blur,
The time is twelve, or 11, or 10?
Electron pulses through circuitry to bend.

Tiny Little Boats

Oh, I almost forgot; I want to tell you,
Things that I thought I almost knew,
Those precious facts to help me relax,
As I go with the flow; forward to go back,
Direction spinning around, focusing ahead,
Stopping only to see it is all I've said,
A day surprisingly unknown in nature,
Yet I can feel my soul steadily mature,
Selecting angles to view thoughts shown,
Abstract changes consistent; almost known,
To rearrange the time spent thinking of her,
As my mind may very easily concur,
My independence & way of approach,
I'll try to keep afloat our tiny little boats.

Enjoying this World

Quick turn away, you know how,
It was scary, but you know now,
Anger and misery is not what you want,
Search for good times, back to the hunt,
You deserve to feel good; only the best,
Discard the bad, to now rest,
It took energy & courage, but there's more,
Your view is now a wide open door,
Step through into a knowing of a new you,
Please know this and it will be true,
A person capable of enjoying this world,
So much more than ever before,
I can see in you a glimmer so bright,
Thank you for being this shining light.

Arriving by Day Light

A clever play on a vocabulary of words,
Describe a noun, & then add a verb,
Yet, honestly, is there any substance?
The value of recognizing what this is,
Authentic ways can be living a truth,
As a tightened grip, works its way loose,
Leaning into one way or the other,
Questioning my intention, so why bother?
Doubt & disbelief witness receptiveness,
More unknowns of consciousness,
It would be nice to create through thought,
Contemplative selection revises if it is not,
Can my soul search though out the night?
Peace, then, arrives by day light.

I Realize

A thought, to a word, to the next,
Of what is nothing more; nothing less,
Contemplating on what I could lose,
Taking action on the path I'll choose,
It takes away from what to say to you,
Within days it is now something new,
When an opportunity in now distant,
I'll turn to myself to be consistent,
Nobody is coming to save me,
Yet I realize what will be,
The strength I have in myself,
My inner being and inner wealth,
I know I can do this today,
Non-resistant type of action is the way.

Smashed Cell Phone

Hardware connected to a network within air,
Annoying cell phone smashed without care,
Soon no more of the circuitry's energy,
This happens with a non-working battery,
To contemplate a digital signal with wit,
Where and when is the last invisible bit?
Information; translation; silly wave particle,
Of course I know this poem is maniacal,
Space-time coordinates, the last bit of data,
Somewhere in the air? What is it made of?
I need to know if I swallowed that bit,
This little bit of data could be a perfect fit,
Through the atomic clock as a basis of time,
My mind is baffled in this scientific rhyme.

Playing the Villain

To be the villain, the evil, the bad,
To be the one who is sad,
If a person decides that is who they are,
They will go nowhere, and they'll go far,
I want to help and give what I offer,
While it is illogical to suffer,
Together we can boost our confidence,
Regardless of having more or having less,
A relative term known as better,
Compared to me, or anyone of these letters,
Or these words, or this poem,
So they think within their knowing,
Passing through the perspective showing,
We can overcome the stages of growing.

Clockwork Variable

Organization is found; precision is attained,
Yet so is a variable to question my brain,
The unknown time of my love,
Not even to be predicted by the stars above,
Her free spirit & wondrous travels,
Logic & theory completely unravel,
Understanding, & communication is nice,
When the same thing never happens twice,
She is a mystery in the form of a woman,
In the many situations as I go through them,
Catch my breath & continue in admiration,
No tests to pass, as to avoid a graduation,
Only fun & enjoyment of life today,
She brightens the world in a unique way.

Narrow Gate

Despite an approach based on fear,
Intention revealed & made perfectly clear,
At a point where I can finally see,
The best form of interaction for me,
Dreams verging; nightmare characteristics,
Please wake up & realize life's logistics,
Surrender to something within who I am,
Sitting on a beach; countless grains of sand,
Deciphering common sense about choices,
I will tune out their actions & voices,
To once again be confident & free to live,
As much as I try to help & give,
This is for you to learn & maybe escape,
Awareness leads through a narrow gate.

A New Vision

The resistance to a hope or a dream,
To honestly feel I deserve good things,
To give my life and this world a chance,
It will only be my loss if I take a glance,
Of the way I want things to be,
To turn around to a view I want to see,
They are there waiting, and better yet,
They are around me now, without regret,
I can move forward with a life to live,
If I close myself off, I cannot easily give,
Something I want so much to do,
The only way I know how to express to you,
I've always had the key to my own prison,
It's time to open the door to a new vision.

Thought Selection

Rationing movements through a time span,
Steps to a situation; chosen consciousness,
Changing occasionally as the eyes blink,
Transforming the experiences,
Guided by thought selection,
Extra energy behind the intention,
Toward the path I want,
Seizing the opportunity to plan,
Events couldn't happen any other way,
A blueprint of the directions to go,
Priorities within a decision to approach,
The past & future versions of who I am,
Communicate within the unity of my mind,
Accepting responsibility for what is now.

This Path

Continuing on this path of compassion,
As the time, is divine, with intervention,
A universe within selection of words given,
Starting to initialize the new perception,
To cancel the projected view of what is,
Opening & closing doors; the life is his,
Feeding a story of silence & clarity,
The resetting of what is defined of as variety,
Secrets revealed, questions, & purpose,
Cleverly choosing the story through this,
A hidden truth within familiar faces,
At least to see it, surrounding these places,
The dreams solve subconscious messages,
It leads me throughout the many passages.

Scenario of Observation

(Through Many Situations)

Interwoven Connection

As we move through life & grow,
The interwoven connection we may know,
If everything at once was shown,
Would I consider myself to be alone?
There is something to look forward to,
As in the next time I will see you,
The many times that I wonder,
What you are thinking & what you ponder,
When we talk, there are usually few words,
Conversational music; the singing of birds,
I would like our relationship to grow fonder,
The times I think of you as I wonder,
Many thoughts are hidden in my mind,
To be revealed at a later time.

Unfold & Display

I wonder about a situation unknown,
A pen and paper in front of me shown,
The days of hope that this will continue,
When I feel fresh, clean, and brand new,
Awake & aware, soft warm breeze in the air,
Alive & free, without worry or care,
A time to let down my guard; I didn't know,
The innocence of the heart it may show,
Childhood play & what I would say,
In remembering that day, I just want to stay,
This world can be wonderful if I allow,
I can always choose to rearrange the now,
So onto the next phase of life today,
Letting the world unfold and display.

A Careful Truth

Invested learning to apply toward this,
What could possibly be continuous bliss?
Curious about these feelings at times,
A point where it all seems to align,
The lessons life has offered until today,
To help us know a path & a way,
Towards an experience with each scenario,
Moving with us in the way a thought goes,
Yet, I know what's right,
So that's why I write,
Glowing vibe & essence; a smile to share,
Expression with the way I truly can care,
With this, & that; with faith & time,
I am thankful for the ability to rhyme.

Options Selected

A divine source is always guiding us,
For this reason I have complete trust,
Through doorways into the future,
Angels around us with all things pure,
An adventure of this known love,
As I gaze at the stars above,
Focusing toward what my eyes can see,
The possibilities branch out, as if on a tree,
Options selected & memories collected,
All of this our God has directed,
Conscious thoughts of what is now here,
Surrounding environment; so far, yet near,
Enjoyment moving forward with ease,
In the way this happens for you & for me.

Time in Formation

As I think about what was told,
Many words & actions, as we get old,
Yet with a soft spoken voice,
I know we always have a choice,
Step by step toward a destination,
Gratitude for the current situation,
Preference leans towards a favorite,
So it is time again to celebrate,
The preciousness of each moment,
All that it holds within it,
Night & day; time in formation,
Stories passed along as if in circulation,
As mystical vapor forms in the air,
All this is cherished, sacred, unique, & rare.

A Home in Heaven

Doing this to honor someone else,
Infinite patience negating the jealous,
Dedication; waiting when contemplating,
The best I can do without complicating,
What is most important in life while here?
Gratitude & thanks for all I hold dear,
With this thought to serve others,
The needs that reveal what was covered,
Governing laws surround to obey,
10 Commandments & the rest of the day,
Caring, understanding, loving, & forgiving,
A truth this world is consistently revealing,
A wonderful world; a home in heaven,
Life is miraculous as it surrounds within.

How Things Are

Divine intervention & timing will guide,
There is no reason for my emotions to hide,
I look forward to the good times we'll share,
I hope you realize about how much I care,
When a focus throughout the day will show,
The way I truly want things to go,
I'll try my best & send you my love,
A peace within, around, below, & above,
All things good will arrive to you today,
I want to affirm that I am thankful as I pray,
As for what is now, & how things are,
I will do my best while you are away so far,
God please send her to be by my side,
These are feelings of an adventurous ride.

Reflective Response

Thank you for the understanding & freedom,
Alone, my best friend; I know who I am,
With the way it is & what I want to be,
The way I am & what you need from me,
As we are connected through time & space,
At times we are both in the same place,
Mutual expectations within these situations,
Learning to be; peace within patience,
Focused; thoughts about our relationship,
Many people going with the flow of it,
Resistance is persistent, if not allowed,
Please stay in this eternal time of now,
The past, a story; the future, a dream,
Scenarios change with what words bring.

The Thoughts Involved

A forward pattern circles eternity,
Forever moving with & through purity,
Within the soul, behind the ego's disguise,
Peace of mind & the kingdom arrives,
Transfer change; contemplate innocence,
The middle starts towards words like this,
A next step shown within a sequence,
Good feelings revealed for times of bliss,
Steps toward the smoothing of resistance,
Conscious mind; the thoughts are consistent,
Position realigned for an original path,
How can a riddle be solved with math?
Amazing production; constructing to watch,
A seed, water, soil, & the sunlight caught.

Unknown Expectations

Within this perspective; this view,
I have no doubt what to do,
Whether rejection or acceptance,
How it's meant to be has kept this,
There is always another way,
Keeping an open mind in what I say,
An expansion of possibilities,
My molecules; a vibe in frequency,
With what dreams are made of,
Yet, I focus on reality, because,
That is where I can create,
My thoughts, my path, & my fate,
To fine tune my enjoyment,
Where it is & where it went.

Guided & Protected

I may not understand why all this is,
I've been guided & protected through this,
I am still here to write this poem,
For right now here is my home,
Simple words, an essence to know,
This takes me in the way it will go,
I feel that regardless or with regard,
I can make this easy or hard,
If I want I can connect to enjoy,
If I want I can create or destroy,
Selecting with care my actions on a thought,
Applying what life lessons have taught,
To write this & do what I can,
Has this all made me who I am?

Repeated Patterns

How could I prevent repeated patterns?
Of what to me really matters,
The things I hold sacred each day,
To not worry about what I'll do or say,
To not look back & embrace the past,
Rather to look forward, to make it last,
Conscious movement in what I'm doing,
As I try to continue with what I'm pursuing,
If irrational or paranoid thought returns,
I'll identify it & address the concern,
Focusing on all that is now,
Maybe the way to figure out how,
It may seem that is the way,
Simply put, today is today.

Inertia to Create

There is a way to view life just as it is,
Direction or place in that or this,
I'm finding it's true what they say,
No matter where I go, there I am today,
It seems there is something needed,
Without it I feel depressed & depleted,
To follow my bliss, purpose, & passion,
Not avoiding it in an ordinary fashion,
Rather to take control & do what I love,
Just as an astronomer looks at the sky above,
The choice of doing what I enjoy,
Hiring myself with this job I employ,
Inertia of moving consistently to create,
I embrace the moment, the day, & my fate.

What Will Be

Getting involved in the world I live,
There is a way that I may give,
Keeping away from thoughts too addictive,
During the times I feel indecisive,
I signed up for one of life's lessons,
My struggle of letting go of possessions,
My request became something true,
Caring enough to let things be with you,
The experience I learned from,
When I thought it was all coming undone,
It was a blessing, so I now know,
This is the way it will go,
A soothing effect on how things are,
Yet knowing I must continue to travel far.

At Any Time

Looking back at the thoughts I believed,
Rather depressing & myself I deceived,
I made a choice in a pattern of thought,
Instead of romance; loneliness I bought,
I chose to focus on what I didn't have,
Obviously this made me very sad,
Now that I've identified this, I need action,
To know & believe in complete satisfaction,
To forgive myself for believing those things,
If I don't, it will continue to be,
I want to realize what is right,
To enjoy, to prosper, to live a happy life,
All of this is available to me at any time,
To always enjoy each moment I find.

Finding a Question

Too quick, slow it down,
Not realizing what's all around,
I know I have options,
With what I have thoughts on,
Taking time to relax & think,
Slowly pouring what I drink,
Finding a question of yes or no,
Hoping & praying that I know,
Holding on by letting go,
To see what reality will show,
Clearing the obstacles, for the good of all,
The day they will eventually call,
Ring, ring; answer it now,
I guess I'm unsure to question how.

Conceptual Twists

A view in which I can see them,
Opportunities appear & doors open,
Word structure with phase changes,
Conceptual twists & time phases,
All of the other curiously interesting ways,
To occupy a moment throughout the day,
Ok, just a few seconds ago,
Something I can't describe, yet I know,
With the essence of the source,
Channeling the capability of course,
Just letting things move as I let them go,
A direction I've chosen within the flow,
Why would I want to pursue that again?
The consistency of now is soon to be then.

Same River Twice

A philosophical question, that is oh so nice,
Can a person step in the same river twice?
If the river is named it can be done,
Yet original water molecules make it fun,
Different water from around the world,
Consistently spinning with twirls,
A changing view; who I am & the life I live,
The eternal changing life God gives,
A whole new view of what things are,
Naming it for stability, if this goes too far,
If I really want change; a particular flow,
A truth in perception, & a way I'll know,
A stream, with water, or shifting formation,
All is within the perspective of a definition.

Neutral Ground

Contemplating within a neutral ground,
Human nature in silence, no sound,
Coming together to relate to it all,
Climb real high, or decide to fall,
Beneath the majority & a truth to tell,
Looking back now, I hope that I fell,
To the calmness & peace underneath,
Knowing who I am to find my relief,
Worthy of others to project a thought,
What something is & what it is not,
Precious love, please hold me down,
Without the within, forward, & around,
These small pieces expand throughout,
Centering in balance; leveled in the now.

Psychological Time

With faith I hope for life to arrive,
I have to admit, I'm the one to decide,
To give life in physical form a chance,
I've learned of the non-physical dance,
I interact in society the best I can,
To know life & to know who I am,
Am I wrong in the assumptions I think?
As I sit, taking sips, of the coffee I drink,
That's probably it, I analyze everything,
This shows a frictional way of being,
One thing leads to another in a smooth way,
How the time moves throughout the day,
Of course time moves forward on a clock,
Psychologically it is a boat with no dock.

Visualize a Dream

Within a moment, things are in control,
Then out of control & on a roll,
Swept away, yet, with faith & trust,
Knowing what I can't change, yet I must,
It's not my job to do so,
I try my best to let God & let go,
In the bigger picture I may see,
A perspective to relax & let things be,
What happens today has possibility,
Thankful for what is taken care of for me,
Visualize a dream, & look forward,
In what I most want to move toward,
Shifting into the wonderful view,
I look forward to spending time with you.

Small Steps

I'll take small steps toward larger goals,
It seems to be the best way I know,
At times, motivation can be a difficulty,
Defining what that truly means to me,
For too long, there was a time period,
To make a change, or face the fear of it,
I want to identify where I went astray,
To take action with progress in a way,
While in the past, my conscience took a toll,
A way in the world; what my mind told,
Ironically that's what I worried about,
Avoiding the task, my head in the clouds,
I'll make a long story short, of course,
All things emanate from a wonderful source.

Conformity & Silence

While I interact with society,
I wonder, what is the right way to be?
I notice certain people will go with the flow,
Or use their silence to hide what they know,
Not with an unusual question or action,
Rather to gain their satisfaction,
Am I searching for the truths of the world?
This crazy little planet spins & twirls,
Is there somewhere else we all know?
The infinite realms of heaven is where to go,
Surrender to the Creator of life,
I may just find my beloved wife,
For now I'm just learning about myself,
Opportunities bloom in wise inner wealth.

Commitment

There is a goal, a dream, a way to be,
I don't want other things to distract me,
I find throughout the day I go,
A focus during the time I know,
It's quite easy actually, once I identify,
What I want & to not worry why,
Following a vision of what I know is right,
Re-align when my focus is off site,
Honor what I feel is special to me,
Using time, awareness, & energy,
Respecting what I give great value,
Commitment to what I feel is true,
The relationship I want to have with you,
I sincerely want to do the best I can do.

Dreams of Now

Embracing courage to allow this to be,
What it truly is, I may be able to see,
I tend to assign a label to how I think,
The ingredients of the beverage I drink,
Experience a taste, not to be categorized,
Allowing to savor; to be mesmerized,
Whether five minutes or five hours,
Any thought we relate to is ours,
Beliefs between the times I ponder,
I daydream, meditate, and wander,
To not know and be okay regardless,
When beginning, no matter how far it is,
Dreams of now, wishes of my desires,
As the sun rises & the night retires.

Hiding My Dark Side

Something just doesn't feel right,
Internal morality is the fight,
I feel like I'm holding on,
Fears of my possession being gone,
Those things I should set free,
When none of this was meant for me,
Feeling the shame of my insecurity,
Creating my own plan egotistically,
Being real with fear itself,
Not knowing the true definition of wealth,
Is it possible to understand love?
For myself this means God above,
Hoping for an optimistic visual,
Knowing of my dark side's residual.

Intuitive Feelings

It seems I needed logic,
To realize I don't need logic,
To surrender, let go, & not worry,
Rationalizing my actions of hurry,
Or a relaxed pace where I allow it to be,
When the solution now arrives to me,
What intuitively feels to be the next step?
Let go of the emotional baggage I kept,
Do I need to struggle for a reason?
Change & growth through life's seasons,
A forward movement starts the ball rolling,
Release a thought; my mind was controlling,
It progressively makes this the best it can be,
An intellectual door, opened with a key.

Unity & Separation

Gather together & hold tight with faith,
Unified time & space will not separate,
Equations of equal, greater, or less than,
Yet human equality is possible; we can,
A mind may struggle in emotion & thought,
Through a balance of what is & what's not,
Work together to evaporate what separates,
It's only natural to give & to take,
Although it's not easy at times for optimism,
A challenge to practice it with discipline,
A cycle forward; movement in growth,
Relocation of what the here & now is worth,
Perception, perspective, & description,
I'll follow my heart with love & conviction.

Experiences of a Day

As I listen to the wisdom internally,
Interacting with what happens externally,
Visualizing what overall is the rest of today,
Remembering the choices of yesterday,
They connect to accumulate this way,
The actions I take & the words I say,
The thoughts I entertain in my brain,
Interactive expression is the game,
Taking responsibility in what I create,
For myself & others, with what is my fate,
Not victimized, when acting on my behalf,
As to find a sense of humor & to laugh,
This all adds up to what unfolds as my day,
An entire life connected in what I display.

Patience & Forgiveness

At times I'm not who I want to be,
When clear & rational thinking I cannot see,
Human emotion includes anger & sadness,
It seems I cannot always keep my happiness,
Not intentionally making that choice,
I want to recognize this as part of my voice,
Lessons of a realization still growing,
Within me there is still a knowing,
Nobody is perfect, is that an excuse?
If I'm at war with myself, I need a truce,
To be gentle with the mistakes made,
Life continues on, as the oceanic waves,
Patience & forgiveness of myself & others,
Emotion ranges like a spectrum of colors.

Emotional Navigation

To find my way in the journey each day,
Not all maps do what they say,
Yet if I was to use a compass & know,
My emotional navigation will help me go,
I recognize the thoughts I am thinking,
Metaphorically if I'm floating or sinking,
What I want & how I interact,
I'm fairly sure this is scientific fact,
Regardless, there is something to be said,
The wise inner voice in my head,
Not the same as a fast racing thought,
Calm awareness is a clarity that's caught,
As I want good relationships with others,
I can then realize the territory it covers.

Formation of Water

Water can be expressed in different ways,
Scientific or throughout linguistic arrays,
Created, destroyed, a change in formation,
Ice or vapor, with the potential of creation,
Variables give a clue of the temperature,
It is what it is; in a vague way I'm sure,
The indescribable life water gives us,
Properties held, in which we trust,
It's fascinating & I often think,
I recognize this when I take a drink,
Enlightened gratitude; step back & observe,
How much of nature will be conserved?
A snowflake, steam, or merely a storm,
It is who we are in physical form.

Transmit & Receive

I'll transmit words, from thought to paper,
An attempt to love myself as my neighbor,
Frequency of sound behind the meaning,
Tuning into a visualized way of dreaming,
Received as a feeling, follow this thought,
To know what I'm thinking & what I'm not,
An unobserved signal sent out in possibility,
Faith may determine if it is synchronicity,
Step back to view the big picture,
The wisdom I've learned from scripture,
A perspective of what this world is,
My reality is balanced by what I give,
In expectation of a future scenario,
Moving forward to find out where this goes.

Momentarily Waiting

Time within the mind is where I'll focus,
Only what is referred to as hocus pocus,
If I entertain & run with a thought,
Instead of always referring to a clock,
Yet thinking clearly & loving dearly,
Understanding this is important to me,
Recognize what's around & within,
Who am I & where have I been?
Here, there, & everywhere,
With unconditional or traditional care,
Oh well, what I've attempted to tell,
I'll slow down & admit that I fell,
In love, in word, & in motion,
Natural life is the magical potion.

Understand the Catalyst

To define what the sound creates,
Is not how to understand what it negates,
It is a blessing of timing & realized silence,
When understood it will create a resilience,
From one to the next, then, back to the first,
A moment just started, yet ends with a birth,
Existing temporarily without knowing,
Behind the physical form that is showing,
Intention invented for frustration prevented,
Connecting to unify; equal sound presented,
Time to simplify, for the lesson was given,
What I learned & where I will be driven,
To the next point in time & place in space,
Erratic pattern understood in style & grace.

Life Information

With courage & a surrender to action,
Life information guides toward an intention,
Angels watch over to guide you,
God orchestrates what's connected through,
Faith interacting within a community,
A support system needed; part of humanity,
To live what I'm capable of, while alive,
The memories of love at a time of goodbye,
Gentle reminders with divine intervention,
Signs throughout the day that God mentions,
A reminder in the experience of this writing,
A situation that puts awareness in sighting,
Overlooking the idea within the blindness,
I will refocus on what is forgiveness.

Self-Trust

Completing a format of what to trust,
It's not required to make this a must,
Rather a suggestion to follow intuition,
As to how I feel about a situation,
A unifying line around silence of mind,
This is hidden within to possibly find,
Knowledge of coincidental events,
Safely rewarding what this prevents,
The best I know how to do,
The heart reveals; moving me though,
Four, three, two, one, just for fun,
Or change the direction to run,
So I can see this is merely a walk,
Intention displayed an informational talk.

Orchestrated Connection

If there was a circuitry of the soul,
Mechanical in the way I was told,
There would be a connection throughout,
Independently & honestly, I have doubt,
A thought moving towards a goal,
Destination paid for with some gold,
A metal made from lyrical alchemy,
As a focused mind moves towards destiny,
Strength of mind to maintain sanity,
Now I can let it go, for what next will be,
Pick up the pieces & continue on,
As this new moment is born,
Within an orchestra's complete unity,
I've been given a mind to play with reality.

Equal Resistance

One way towards the other,
I could find it to be a bother,
If I haven't labeled it as good or bad,
There is no reason to be happy or sad,
To find out what will be continuous,
A circular rotating line of trust,
An expression requires variable intent,
To perceive a view of satisfied content,
One molecular bond against another,
Magnetic forces arrange as the field covers,
In & out of existence, scientifically,
The way it was told to me specifically,
So I'll move through life carefully,
I believe this happens substantially.

An Open Doorway

This might be thought of as the next step,
What the mind let's go of & what is kept,
If there was a doorway to something else,
Would I agree with who I am within myself?
If to open with a key of what's inside of me,
This would allow what could be, to just be,
While the time cycles may continue,
An ordinary pattern of what to do,
Outside of what I've stepped into,
For all that I've been through,
In front of me or behind my view,
There is no key when there is a clue,
What is honestly a good connection?
I can approach a door of thought selection.

PRECIOUS TIME

(Inner Struggle in Rhyme)

Our Friendship

To let you know I appreciate you as a friend,
Regardless; what is a beginning or an end?
Simplicity speaks volumes for me,
Gratitude to just let things be,
Always wanting you to feel free,
Currently this is how I see,
I trust the wisdom you have in what you do,
To support this friendship moving through,
To just comfortably let you know,
I'm glad this is how it will go,
Thank you so much for who you are,
Friendship is precious as the sky & the stars,
For now that's all I can think to say,
Have an enjoyable & wonderful day.

Hesitant Words

I'm hesitant to express what's on my mind,
The words to use now I can't seem to find,
Careful ways of saying what I feel,
Or nothing in my thoughts to reveal,
I could create a story of how things are,
My mind telling me I've gone too far,
Visualize reality; not knowing what I want,
Or maybe I do, & the answer is rather blunt,
What is out of my control seems to be a lot,
Am I letting go & accepting what is not?
I'll seize the moment & take some action,
I offered a distance of silence for reaction,
Too much to say for a short term of time,
A world displayed through abstract rhyme.

Second Chances

For all the times I've fallen,
To express myself seems to be my calling,
I seem to deal with the same situation,
Yet this tight rope has variation,
Perfect a craft; perfect a skill,
Diagnose my faults as to take a pill,
Once again I can face what is ahead,
Ideas & notions my mind has said,
Although I weed out thorns of thought,
There is a debt of choices I have bought,
I'll try my best to follow along,
An awakening to life, or just being gone,
Consciously I'm back to who I am,
Once again this all seems to begin.

Sequential Actions

When the present moment escapes my view,
Thinking of the future to know what to do,
Thinking of the past; played out in my mind,
A gentle gesture of trying to be kind,
Irrational thought forms movies to believe,
Is it my imagination in which I receive?
A logical action is within my reach,
Or just common sense to simplify relief,
Knowing I'm doing what I can to let it be,
Motivating forward & knowing what I see,
Visualizing & setting a stage to perform,
For what is not yet, but soon to be born,
The next moment has arrived; now I decide,
Sequential actions are lined up side by side.

Memory Search

As I segment the search of what happened,
I currently don't remember, so what then?
Some way I'll know what to write,
Somehow I'll feed the mouth that will bite,
In the words I put together for a rhyme,
Formulating how to spend my time,
Clarity seems gone & I'm not sure why,
For now I'll acknowledge I can't fly,
Maybe in my dreams as I sleep,
Or if I'm levitating the ideas I seek,
If I could save the villain from the victim,
As it happens, I'll be at peace with him,
For her to be by my side; happily ever after,
Yet, inside my world is temporary laughter.

Talking to the Sky

Outward off the planet, I look above,
To say hello to all that life is made of,
Curiosity & imagination of possibility,
The other side of what is known as reality,
Are you here? Are you there?
The time continuum leads me to stare,
The connection of all things unifies,
So I open my heart & look to the skies,
I can relate to the storms & the worry,
Running through the rain so fast in a hurry,
Smiling & admiring the view of endlessness,
By doing this, it may just be divine bliss,
Whether clouds or stars, black or blue,
It helps me to know what to do for you.

Paradox of Content

The paradox of content confuses my intent,
Many ideas I could try & present,
As pride predicts meaningless conquest,
When all I want to do is rest,
Peaceful eternal slumber within a void,
Always created & never to be destroyed,
An unusual plan is implemented today,
Floating through air in a particular way,
To those who will meet my arrival,
Transcending a view; my eyes of survival,
Sacrificial loss, a cost, & whispered lyrics,
Yesterday is now clenched in my fists,
Lies revealed with a subconscious told,
My pulse is borrowed & now it is sold.

It Never Was

Seemingly the situation is carefully planned,
Expected routines die; spontaneity banned,
Thinking things a certain way ruins them,
Logic escapes when eleven follows ten,
After eleven is twelve; from point to point,
To count the cash or count the coins,
Rehearsed or reversed, life should be alive,
Not knowing if today is the day I die,
It is always now, but that's not new,
At least this time I know what to do,
A form of structure is necessary, sure,
I just don't want to ever be this bored,
The moment is here, what should I do?
Pretend it never was, so it can be new.

Consistent Situation

Consistent situation; flowing options known,
Explanation happening; exactly shown,
Why I did this & how I did that,
Scenario now passed within an online chat,
Competitive edge & negotiation of myself,
Personality differentiates; my soul will tell,
Right in front of me, yet I can't see,
What is truly happening to me?
Bizarre situations; let go of this thinking,
Sitting here with the beverage I'm drinking,
My mind, a blur, then, I open my eyes,
I will survive, as my ego tries,
Surrounding space; let me be free to see,
Therapeutic help within all that could be.

Above My View

Above my view; look at how you grew,
Bigger & better, ground beneath your shoes,
Walking & talking, like a song in the air,
Verses of all the ways there are to care,
Harmonious movements; get it out to vent,
That's all it is & all that I meant,
A system of culture & society,
The ability & right to do this is free,
Or in other words of lecture & speech,
What I could learn & what I could teach,
Anyway, if this state of mind continues,
Still a constant, when change is what's true,
In my pocket I have something of weight,
Description of that, may affect my fate.

Nothing to Say

Bite my lip, my mind is quiet,
No need to do what could cause a riot,
Which part of my personality wants to talk?
Why is stillness how I should walk?
Silent contemplation in this situation,
A subjective tense; here & now in position,
Power over others I do not have,
It's enough to be me & to be glad,
Others living their life & their business,
So I'll do something with mine, I guess,
Knowing what I'm able to do is a start,
Emerging together, yet so far apart,
The cause is clear with an affect by God,
For now I'll agree & simply nod.

Sleepless Night

I wonder; I worry; I try my best,
Of what is enjoyment & not even a test,
Fatigue, then a deep breath, I'm okay,
Focused toward what I want to say,
It's a story I'm telling my mind,
The thoughts that my reality finds,
It's now, so I have this time,
To do my best to skillfully rhyme,
The time moves quickly, I enjoy what I do,
So much easier of a way to go through,
Options & selections, striving for perfection,
Knowing that I am following a direction,
An hour to go, just the current moment,
Deciding to support it, or condone it.

Disappear

Right now I just want to disappear,
Hide in the invisible from all I fear,
What I say to you & others,
What I say to sisters & brothers,
It doesn't seem like its ever good enough,
Thoughts to haunt, which makes this tough,
I know who I am, so I shouldn't believe,
Negativity causes only me to be deceived,
Sitting here calmly writing these words,
My mind is in a war over something absurd,
A panic attack, so I brace for the storm,
It may take a while to return to the norm,
Before I know it, things are good,
Thoughts disappear, in the way they should.

The Day Begins

My eyes open, the day begins,
Looking back & laughing at my sins,
I am not what they think,
So, to get started, it's coffee I'll drink,
Magic realm to overwhelm the unknown,
What is before me is always shown,
A taste of the immortal now,
An essence within to be around,
Yet, to show respect, I'll live,
To take the cause & effect of what I'll give,
Possibilities, limitations, & situations,
What I truly want to be my creation,
The world, environment, with interaction,
I can feel content with a certain satisfaction.

Quick Glances

Waking hours & I pray for rest,
So much easier than breath after breath,
A scattered format of thoughts to offer,
Not knowing if I could trust her,
This doubt can only do its worst,
A blessing recognizes the end of a curse,
Expand throughout this guarded light,
Guiding, protecting, & taking flight,
Divinity within represents a tree & a book,
Recovering the quick glances of a look,
I tremble in this struggle to hold on,
To have faith there was a reason I was born,
Apologetic for me even being alive,
Acknowledge the inevitability that I will die.

Perspective of Problems

I'm lucky to be alive,
I'm blessed I haven't yet died,
I'm thankful I'm not jailed,
I'm glad the harm against me failed,
There are some with a diagnosis,
Symptoms of the mind to know this,
Some are homeless, others are dead,
Yet I can write this to be read,
To celebrate how much I've overcome,
My life is not yet over or done,
Compassion, mockery, pain, or laughter,
Then arrives the calm with a storm after,
We all have problems to deal with,
Content of character pulls me through this.

Passive Approach

I try to resist what I fear the most,
Passive approach, heaven sent; not to boast,
All good & decisive, a taste of life to savor,
Fluent flavors of good & bad behavior,
Mentally, I have a penny, & that's plenty,
No longer us; nothing between you & me,
Look around as gravity stills the ground,
Beats & rhythms helping the sound,
No news; good news; through & through,
Written for you & the pursued is now due,
Respect with delivery in all I see,
Only because this is the way I need to be,
Continuing to browse for what is mine,
Not necessarily egotistical with what I find.

Focused Choice

Fine-tuned temptations toward them,
Designed to break commandments of ten,
Heart beats per second; counted,
Funds deposited in the way amounted,
Seven, six, five, four, three, two, one,
With salvation through a victory won,
Defeated enemy, deception of a liar,
Scorching flames of eternal fire,
Bye for now, hello, & so it goes,
The eternal end of how a river flows,
Breaking into realms, pass by in walking,
Gossip, judgment, coveting, & talking,
Walking the path of what is before me,
Branches connect; symmetric roots of a tree.

Erratic Clutter

A normal vibe in the room tonight,
Making progress with the inertia I fight,
Talk it out, keep writing some words,
Eventually I'll make it through the absurd,
Could I describe certain meaning like that?
It must be where my perspective is at,
At some point I have to let go,
Hopefully new things will show,
Cleaning out forms of erratic clutter,
Streams, sewers, rivers, & gutters,
Sort this out to find a means to relax,
Belief in myself & sticking to the facts,
Conclusion arrives, yet I'm not done,
When will this end, to again see the sun?

A Mistake

It's really not a surprise,
You can see it in my eyes,
There is no one else to blame,
In my own world, all the same,
To approach me now would be a mistake,
Not much of a relationship to make,
I've brought this upon myself,
Emotional currency equals zero wealth,
I don't trust who I am, & I don't trust you,
No wonder this is what I'm going through,
This mental story will keep distance,
Keep me lonely for only an instance,
One thought away, toward a new direction,
I do have a choice & a form of selection.

Formula of Files

Searching for a pattern known,
I look at the numbers shown,
I know it exists with an exponential amount,
A formula of files that I try to count,
Groups within a descending array,
Mathematically ascending the opposite way,
It is a mere illusion with a simple pattern,
Binary numbers; will others count them?
A path to follow to arrive at the destination,
I probably created it for need of a vacation,
I tried to confuse to keep something safe,
To make it special in a hidden place,
So now I've tried to explain,
I feel this is all very simple & plain.

One Kind

If to ruin a chance to prove this false,
Boundaries in a maze of music for cost,
Shifting shapes & a standard form,
Temporarily keeping the idea yet born,
God knows & the ground beneath is still,
To be rewarded in the morning with a pill,
My own business from the previous rain,
Supporting the idea of leaving the pain,
A new idea with a cozy surface,
Deception of confidence to almost blur this,
A stream of light, no data included,
Five minutes corrupts what is polluted,
Bring forward a birth of what will be,
I'll regard the life that was brought to me.

Bringing Me Back

A low feeling of the same thought again,
I can make a new choice, but when?
I could think I'm spiritual & pure,
Yet what if I don't know & I'm not sure,
I really don't know what to do,
A repeated pattern I go through,
Bringing me back to where I started,
As hope for better days has departed,
Is there still time to turn this around?
A subtle glimpse of possibilities found,
How can I maintain forward progress?
If this is a lesson or one of life's tests,
I'll pray for authentic words to write,
I'll try to be gentle with myself tonight.

Escape from Reality

A disc to be viewed or heard,
Some people like this or think it's absurd,
Clear the mind; deep breaths,
Clarity for a time to stop & confess,
A movie's plot playing in my thoughts,
A routine of what is real & what is not,
The less it is about me, the better off I'll be,
Stand my ground & focus to be set free,
Avoid imagination to know this,
To regain a simple life of bliss,
This day, this moment, & what surrounds,
Eyes for sight & ears for sound,
I'll take control of my mind & realize,
As escape from reality is what they buy.

Currently

A good attitude, patience, & an afternoon,
Not knowing if something will happen soon,
Can this turn around into something good?
A way to do or say what I know I should,
God give me strength & show your mercy,
To only know how to survive this currently,
Walking at a pace of tension, anger, & rage,
Overly dramatic being rescued from a cage,
I know what I could & should do,
Yet I don't, I resist, & I refuse,
Being alive as my mind scrambles ahead,
Within my head the voices have said,
Just a thought, so relax & try,
It's all in the mind, where I can confide.

Story of a Spider

The webs you've spun,
The end of your life is now done,
Yet in the next phase you'll be fine,
It was only a matter of time,
Waiting while you were deciding,
The instinctive ways you were hiding,
Revealed to know you were there,
Was it because I thought of a scare?
Magnificent creation, its beauty natural,
Insect's dread as you caught them all,
Or maybe the cycle is complete,
A computer term known as delete,
Roaming around the home you knew,
A dimensional portal now traveled through.

Yes or No

To truly know what to do or say,
Unconditional love can show a way,
Yet the doubt in confident habits,
A fear of the unknown future within it,
I think of myself, I think of others,
A reflective nature revealed & covered,
Motivation stops, when its courage I lack,
How can I continue to arrive or get back?
Toward times when it goes smoothly,
No friction with the way life moves me,
The life cycles show this isn't always true,
When I don't do what I want to do,
To possibly relax & go easy with choice,
A simplistic yes or no is an action of voice.

You Knew

Did I realize I was looking down?
There were some boundaries set around,
To avoid some kind of anything,
With an alarm insisting & a sound to bring,
At least I broke free, yet you knew,
A glare to a gaze & a desire to continue,
Twisted pathways seem to straighten out,
Entertaining the notion of what it's about,
When a thought creates this other realm,
Mental movies of stories; form of film,
Voices stop & the stage reveals,
Complete agreement, while making deals,
When the third attempt is obvious enough,
I'll continue to hide & describe more stuff.

Creative Response

To think as a creator & respond as such,
Instinctive reaction may not do as much,
When transcending to higher consciousness,
While living & following continual bliss,
Strive to establish a grasp of the impossible,
A gift is now within the understandable,
If others respond, yet I don't recognize,
Acknowledging a judgment if they criticize,
Rather think of who I am for what it is,
On my own journey, as I pass my own quiz,
No better than you, to just make progress,
Sent into the future with a form of success,
Inner world radiates around my view,
It guides & helps me enjoy what I do.

Definition of Self

If the definition of self is expressed,
Would you define it in a way to impress?
If money talked, by giving to receive,
Does intelligence give to deceive?
The role I display to others for a reaction,
Forms of inertia will push towards an action,
Cause and affect; respect of all I neglect,
Focus for the view of the mind to collect,
More than I can deal with, so I'll relax,
Unstable structure in motion of a collapse,
Brought into form, hopefully preserved,
Maintain its stability & integrity deserved,
Observed & moved to another view,
Unless continued; it's something to do.

Illusion & Romance

I did; they left & the others aren't here,
Opposing what is subsequent & near,
A poem; for at one point they knew him,
The blood flows through the body given,
Veins directed in misunderstood correction,
Unfolding material for a form of protection,
Never flipped; straight static for all,
Another silent scenario & no one to call,
The options must be waited on; for & from,
Unfortunately I'm close to being done,
Time waits for no man; open time to write,
A misleading way to fight my way to flight,
Concluding where silence is a dare,
This romance attaches to nothing there.

Scenario within Time

If forgiveness is granted, I won't attach,
To mix & match & a throw to catch,
Obsession switched in movement away,
I'm trying to focus on what I can say,
The entire human pulse, global & changing,
Intuitive vibe of consistency rearranging,
Chemistry set; marked & ready to go,
Vile of potion distributed to who we know,
Antidote persuaded to cope for the moment,
All too often it leaves with no one to own it,
Broken clock of time, correct in assuming,
Compelled to do what is asked of me,
I guess it boils down as evaporation occurs,
A scenario presented frequently as a blur.

Gratitude for Understanding

As I turned to the left in a reactive fashion,
The tedious idea of what to spend cash on,
Boredom & excuses; revoked & disputed,
I don't know what the root is,
This problem is thought of that way,
Or it could just be another thing to say,
For a balance so crucial to understanding,
Why I'm thankful I have a safe landing,
To observe what is happening here,
For a vantage point of applause & cheer,
Letting go; so it is easy to focus with,
In other words, I remember my wish,
From the time I saw that memory,
In a dream state opened to all that will be.

Breathing Room

Another day for what is according to a start,
The fine-tuned lyrics without forms of art,
When heart can be thought of as soul,
Where inspiration politely pays the toll,
Again with the questions & quotes,
All of the paper filled with musical notes,
Yet not for the benefit of the life I live,
So take nothing into account to finally give,
Surround me & feel less of what's finished,
Increasing the many things that diminish,
Hold this away from the intent seen,
To someday simplify all that I mean,
A message of hope, with ashes & smoke,
Recreating a form once shattered & broke.

So Soon Surrounded

The way it appears to feel compelled,
Listening carefully to the story they tell,
Cautious & curious in what's surrounding,
A choice to accept what life is offering,
When a fact changes before I know it,
This paradox ironically written for a tiny bit,
With affection towards the time of noon,
Color selection; structures of a balloon,
Fragile power operates around the fool,
Ice cold, kind of warm, or maybe just cool,
Celebrations mingle in collaboration,
Strong relations need a good foundation,
If only to continue without worry,
The time is due, yet I'll try not to hurry.

Sunrise

Start, pause, rise, & surprise,
Direction of rotation with metallic eyes,
Reflection of a mirrored optimism,
A new beginning with this kind of baptism,
Rare occasion, yet I'll prepare a meal,
Hungry to the point I feel I want to steal,
I really don't know, but how could I?
Too many ways to perceive a truth or a lie,
So I'll try to make the most of simplicity,
Hoping that it's a good thing I'll see,
Transforming into what is now & here,
Spectrum of light on the horizon so clear,
The solution doesn't have to be solved,
Many trees hold onto the time of fall.

Moment of Mercy

Select a song to sing for love,
Collect the symbols of below & above,
A gift given, honored, & shown,
Still here, with infancy grown,
Show compassion & light,
Clear the mind to see with true sight,
Of varying ways & simple days,
Consistent, parallel, & a form that arrays,
Attempt; visualize, & think positive,
Continue, hope, & just live,
All this & more, after an opened door,
Eternal movement guesses for more,
Conceptually, what does the past mean?
Clarity is how it may be seen.

Ironic Compatibility

With the ability to find a sense of humor,
To acknowledge a question of what it's for,
In other words, it's possible to be breathless,
So let go, follow flow, but don't be reckless,
Too many loose ends & not enough days,
To be patient within a reason of many ways,
To help the helpless, yet less is more,
Freedom to window shop at any fine store,
Or the highway of mysterious vanity,
Virtue escapes the idea of marrying me,
Oh so great, yet not so humble,
In other words, stop pouring when it's full,
To go back & correct what I said,
It can't be taken back by what you just read.

Number of One

The view I see is of just one,
Made up of parts of course, for fun,
To complete, confuse, amuse, & present,
Just more ink on paper for me to vent,
A single amount of binary,
The perspective behind eyes to see,
The point is this; completely missed,
Solitary mental noise as to only resist,
Into a commercial confusion with four points,
Predictable as the politician they appoint,
Forward & backward; a direction to choose,
The kitchen has many things to use,
Big ideas within the circuitry of what's told,
Find the path or merely reinvent the role.

A Million Miles

Situations try to hide their disguise,
I know a truth within all this to arise,
Intuitive steps to take care of a hunger,
Pouring rain, lightening, & thunder,
Assuming perspective presents deception,
Until I realize this clear correction,
One after the other with unconditional ways,
Together the silent thoughts may betray,
A constant that is pure, yet can't be seen,
Occasional prayer of a lifelong dream,
Fragile time for all those mentioned,
With possible conflict prevented,
An opposite direction traveled toward,
To take with me what was absorbed.

CHOICE OF AWARENESS

(A Focus to Decide)

Grace

The transcendence of forgiveness,
Applied to one's personal business,
Knowing I thought of love & kindness,
For myself I thought it was what's best,
It may have been wrong in hind sight,
Divine laws overcome for what grace buys,
So now I realign my focus,
For what intuition & distance can give us,
A new path needed to be experienced,
What I truly want & need within it,
Patience to honor what is now & here,
Gratitude & courage to rise above fear,
So today is a new start for me,
The journey begins from here into eternity.

Thinking Thoughts

What is so wrong with thinking a thought?
I guess it depends on what is & what is not,
Pleasant memories arrive in my mind,
A thought that is encouraging & kind,
Almost as if I need to reach for them,
Yet it feels good to remember when,
Sure, some thoughts are not so good,
Although there is a way that I could,
Search for the times, bringing a smile,
To find peace with my past for a while,
It's good to be in the present moment,
I feel there is no reason to condone it,
Visualization & hope in the future,
Life is a blessing, as we all mature.

Illusion in Experience

Within all that is pure among a broken view,
I'll try to describe the love I have for you,
All that transcends a physical form known,
The illusion in experience, as a gift shown,
Peace, grace, & a life to share one day,
Put into the future with the words I say,
A constant stream of inaccurate perception,
Although I recognize this form of deception,
My finite mind cannot grasp the infinite,
So how could I pretend I am within it?
I'll try to align with divine thought,
To be found humble, yet still I'm caught,
Faith in God, to guide within this dream,
Compassion displays toward what I redeem.

The Road We Choose

When the opposite applies to this,
You may flip the meaning to get the gist,
Although opposites are perfect pairs,
You can travel up or down the stairs,
Arriving at another destination,
The road we choose with hesitation,
A way for understanding & compassion,
More than words, when put into action,
I'll let go of the defined meaning,
The definition will very soon be leaving,
To realize the basic essence of life,
An anniversary of a husband & wife,
Union of opposites may be balanced,
I just wonder if there is a chance.

Change in Choice

Looking back on the past choices I've made,
There is something I recently noticed today,
I've reached a point in a certain way,
To the outer world it is how I'll display,
I no longer do things in how I formerly did,
Kind of like when I used to be a kid,
A sign of maturity through the life I live,
Is this a blessing that God would give?
A breakthrough in the choices I make,
I didn't know how long it would take,
Yet I wanted to make the change,
One day I did from a view point in range,
Even if I look back now into my past,
This will be a change for me that will last.

The Next Form

Leading toward a direction in time & space,
Obstacles, struggles, & challenges we face,
Consistent arrival; physics of consciousness,
Collecting ingredients is a puzzling gift,
Mental wandering, approaches the absolute,
Dwelling of decisions, in hope for the truth,
Surrender intellect for a glimpse once worn,
An object in time, admiring the storm,
Potential experience in an image of energy,
Within my letting go for it to just be,
I've expressed all I can, so where do I go?
I guess as time moves forward I will know,
Relax with faith & hope into the next form,
It emerges with each situation that is born.

Unlocking Life

For a while now, I have collected,
Very keenly & oh so undetected,
Hidden in my mind with each experience,
Tucked away in laughter & seriousness,
I know where each key is located,
As I withdrew & the others debated,
For the knowledge assembled is my vice,
To unlock life in a way that is precise,
So I express to distract the eye,
Waving goodbye, then aligning to say, "Hi",
A gift of invaluable worth in spiritual birth,
Words arrive, deposited in the ocean's surf,
Sands of time, tell me about the beach,
Nature's wisdom will nicely teach.

A Clear Conclusion

Knowledge with an intellect so shallow,
Starting with something I really don't know,
Quiet the mind & take a deep breath,
Take it with me, or should it be left?
Letting it go to attempt a peaceful process,
An outlook harmonizes views in success,
With resolved questions, I feel I belong,
The unknown reveals each word as strong,
With pressure & confusion said honestly,
Yet I'm writing something for it to be,
My reality check to form communication,
A variation in the approach of a situation,
This learning curve kindly faces a fear,
You're not here & the conclusion is clear.

Capture the Idea

It is difficult to find what I'm looking for,
When my view is the same & nothing more,
Recognizing this & looking all around me,
I can try to be open to what I can't yet see,
Defining an improvement; a changing view,
Adaptation of a situation; knowing what to do,
Pulling from out of the air; given to share,
I can capture the idea with care,
Don't worry; it will always be free to go,
I want to honor & show, what I feel I know,
A feeling propels, what seem to be words,
As gliding smoothly; aligning forwards,
If to express how I appreciate these times,
With careful skill, I create some rhymes.

Peaceful Surface

I can't get it right; I can't get it wrong,
I don't know whether to be weak or strong,
It could go either way, if to have a choice,
People with their thoughts, actions, & voice,
Drama, situations, judgments & views,
It's not like any of this is breaking news,
If to keep to myself & try to live in silence,
A battle rages on in my mind with violence,
Turbulent waters; storm of restless arguing,
Treaties, allies, trading, & bargaining,
I'll rise to a unified peaceful surface,
Rather than graph the points of nervousness,
So I labeled what I did as wrong,
Yet, what if I was right all along?

Not There Yet

I can feel it in my soul of being,
There is a certain way of seeing,
I'm not there yet, but I'll know when I am,
To honestly evaluate if I'm a good friend,
With who I am, & with others,
A masquerade that a disguise covers,
I could test the waters so to speak,
Sure, the best view is at the peak,
The highest way of returning so low,
A natural process that life just flows,
I'm grateful for the areas I've improved,
The way my improvement has moved,
Priority of progress, or stay where I am,
The area of focus is what I write with a pen.

Preprogrammed

As synchronize signals manage imagination,
A miraculous healing of this situation,
Welcoming change, colored with emotion,
A moment of growth relating to a notion,
Supporting preprogrammed perspectives,
Within what we bring towards directives,
An intention to create beautiful expression,
Interconnected energy told in confession,
Processing the help of an inspired source,
To safely design a life vision, of course,
A home, not yet perfect, but with potential,
Expanding in the abundance of a sequential,
This connection links the experiences,
Searching for ideas to improve what this is.

Collection

As I surrender to let go & allow,
Thoughts & actions explain to me how,
Intuitively guiding to achieve this goal,
As for a soul's vision to see its focus grow,
I can travel a path to accomplish,
Successful requirements, within this wish,
Assemble the puzzle pieces in collection,
In sharing control of a paradox's direction,
Move the level; balance to prioritize respect,
A onetime experience we all collect,
Unifying the understanding of who we are,
Just reaching for a blessing; it is not too far,
Yet now the current life topic shifts,
So I'll observe the interchangeable for a bit.

Faith to Expect

To expect the best; a constant increase,
Thoughts about this may never cease,
Visualizing wonderful experiences today,
A divine orchestration with the words I say,
More than hope when there is a choice,
Listening to the wise & still, inner voice,
Surrounding an environment of dreams,
Present moment being more than it seems,
This moves toward better & better days,
A map found, out of the complicated maze,
With courage & faith to expect the best,
The excitement leads my life without rest,
I wish these thoughts for you as well,
Sincerely, this is what I will tell.

Planned Thinking

For a complete focus, I will let go,
A choice of awareness to possibly know,
Direction to where I put my attention,
Establishing a present stance of prevention,
I feel that all things are possible,
With the endless unfolding being probable,
The information earned to be applied,
While the situation currently glides,
A deep breath with a prayer of gratitude,
In my sanctuary for a calm attitude,
A divine place with goals & aspirations,
The planned thinking can give preparation,
Alive in the moment, to intuitively feel,
I can apply spiritual tools to what is real.

A Distant View

I have found a reclusive & silent solution,
The world around unfolds with precision,
Clearing the way, by letting go of options,
Circumstances shown, as to watch them,
Let them flow around & through,
A present moment arrival, is what to do,
Well rested with new perspective,
For I don't care about the collective,
Why fake a desire or a dream today?
A self-criticism can radiate in this way,
This judgment defines perfection & control,
A distant view is unnecessary for my soul,
All I see can be simplistic & plain,
The thoughts move as a runaway train.

Reaching

Reaching for better thoughts in my mind,
Sometimes so difficult to find,
Hope applied to knowledge & the unknown,
All of it, in front of me shown,
Delicate power surrounds as I live,
A hazy perspective with an offer to give,
Who I am from dust to dust,
A globe of rebirth & eternal trust,
This truth brings a song to sing,
A universe is birthed as the phone rings,
Although the network connection is old,
I no longer have it to be sold,
Yet I'll look for the blessing,
Emotions open up, to a voice confessing.

Clarify the Confusion

If to create a memory so sweet,
It happens each time we meet,
Beautiful reoccurrence in my mind,
So carefully it will remind,
Sometimes it seems so far away,
An ocean connected, yet far from the bay,
If I knew the meaning of my display,
To others in certain ways today,
Tired & impatient thoughts give me a way,
Human like you, what more can I say?
To be like you & abandon who I am,
Permission grants a capability of how I can,
Stand up, be strong, be who you are,
Clarify the confusion within all this bizarre.

Directed Conversation

The amount of regret I carry,
At times leads life to be scary,
The feelings I hold, connected with thought,
To realize what I am & what I'm not,
A perception of the truth hidden in my past,
If to hold onto it, the memories will last,
If to let it all go & experience this moment,
Directed conversation with life as I own it,
Essence of my soul moving along a path,
Consistency of the zero required for math,
I feel I need to search for something new,
Just to be happy with what is gratitude,
I can only admit with an overwhelmed mind,
To express what currently I'm trying to find.

Patient Love

To validate this way of presentation,
I currently have a kind of sensation,
What is known from my perspective?
Untraceable & hidden to all who will live,
An ancient waiting; simply put for you,
My observation notices something new,
Yes, love, clearing the illusion's view,
Strength increasing as I move through,
Just waiting to be picked from the air,
To prove the way one person can care,
To pave a way & clear a path,
Apply math, count my cash, & take a bath,
Carefully though; they have a trait as well,
Uniquely I present a poem for myself to tell.

Calm Intuition

Looking within my mind to find what is,
Observing what could be of all of this,
Yet intuition tells me to remain calm,
A peaceful voice sings a silent song,
The connection is divine, pure, & authentic,
Actions are sincere in the way I meant it,
Feeding the soul an inspired meal to nourish,
Eternally expanding in how it can flourish,
Not to be labeled & put in a metaphoric box,
An essence of truth without any locks,
A key to all that exists in the world known,
Presenting progression of what has grown,
To be what it is; to be who I am,
I'll add some humor & count to ten.

Another Minute

A machine like pattern moves forward,
A paradox to accomplish tasks as I'm bored,
Sound preparation, planning, & observation,
Is my heart broken from the hesitation?
To see the light of this world's pretense,
Sanity is an opportunity to have a defense,
Who I am; perceiving a presentation,
Throwing away pieces of hope in salvation,
Faith persists to pour energy overflowing,
A divine emotion in a clock work knowing,
This takes me to where I should be,
A temporary delay with a sign I can see,
Decisions & calculations of another minute,
Divide this present moment to begin it.

Temporary & Fragile

These relationships, so temporary & fragile,
Only passing through time for a while,
It directs a focus toward something greater,
When I can't understand & I'm unsure,
Yet I'll trust; I'll limit my questions,
Letting go of surrounding suggestions,
Does fear freeze my quest to choose?
Discerning within a perspective I could lose,
A doubt arrives; I greet it with caution,
The extreme way of safely living begins,
It limits, protects, guides, & hinders,
Narrowing a range of emotion to slender,
My soul steps back to observe,
I'll appreciate the closed doors that occur.

Beyond Now

Present moment moving through,
Connecting of what is into the blue,
God, higher self, source, & universe,
Precise flow to add my own verse,
Who I am, what I offer,
Courage of a question for her,
Authentic intention, life in awareness,
Ask, believe, & receive in consciousness,
Understanding what I want as desire,
Lighting up thought, candle flame of fire,
Opportunity & privilege to be here,
Embracing trust; letting go of fear,
Beyond now, connection of communication,
I'll trust myself, others, & a situation.

Consistent Preference

Bring my inner signals to this place,
Gratitude for small increments of grace,
These overlooked blessings in written form,
An area to start gathering what will be born,
Possible actions; reaching for what's here,
The morning breeze makes it all too clear,
Living my life as they sleep through,
A subconscious state to enjoy & pursue,
Truth in a vision; sights of the unseen,
Passing in time & space; so fresh & clean,
Waiting to serve in a purpose discovered,
Or to be lost, hidden, & cleverly covered,
Please surface a revealed difference,
A regular basis shows consistent preference.

Unknown Answers

How careful do I have to be?
Before I let go & truly see,
Unknown answers to eternal questions,
Learning from others by their suggestions,
Eventually I have to take action,
A spontaneous push; a freeing reaction,
All I can say; All I can do,
In how much I miss being able to see you,
The silence breaks a chosen confusion,
To be warned about other people's illusion,
Technique knows what I hold as important,
In between chaos & disorder that is sorted,
Space has been cleared to continue to write,
The inner fight continues into the night.

What Could Happen?

Observing my thoughts, clearing the mind,
A form of visualization to sometimes find,
Mental stories of how something may be,
Is it realistic to be something I can see?
Sure, there are possibilities unknown,
A prayer of Grace within actions shown,
In all that I do, in silence or sound,
Just in relaxing into what is all around,
Open to experience; discernment is a key,
To decide what is truly important to me,
This form of music is complete & in tune,
What could happen later or very soon?
It is action to recognize the potential,
One at a time unfolds within the sequential.

Prophetic Causality

Systematic story; challenged interpretation,
A mental projection in this situation,
Awakening to a dysfunction of demise,
Generating reality as if in disguise,
Nowhere to go within truth itself,
A separate ego defining the self,
Public danger detaches survival,
When all work as one in arrival,
The unity of text & program source,
Hands full of information of course,
An inevitable claim; vivid determination,
A complete view within manipulation,
Next arrives prophetic causality,
A way to see & a way to be.

Trust in the Continuation

System dividing through a simple rumor,
Society seems to have a sense of humor,
Center the knowing of a plan to think ahead,
Losing focus in words that have been read,
Time spent wisely to dream of tomorrow,
The best I know how; enjoyment or sorrow,
I want to apologize to everyone,
For I am losing many & finding none,
With dedication & faith, I can continue on,
Always alive, I don't remember being born,
This opportunity needs to arrive at the end,
Only so much to do with paper & pen,
Trust in the continuation; this form of hope,
Maybe life is a truth, so I know how to cope.

Honest Hesitancy

To know what is required to avoid a sin,
Regarding the sacrifice involved to begin,
The misleading reward of simplicity in life,
Have I carefully decided to not find a wife?
The tempting complicated life is alluring,
It would be nice if love was a sure thing,
I just hope to one day understand,
Honesty hesitancy, to do what I can,
To recognize a destructive train of thought,
As I overcome thinking to says what it's not,
I hope in the end, for life being kind,
Open to let go, of the rigid thinking I find,
Maybe right now is just not my time,
I'll let go of the idea that anything is mine.

Eternal Glimpse

When accessing salvation to transcend,
Illusion will subjectively meet an end,
Human thought inside a consciousness,
While life pushes forward a process,
Navigate the cryptographic map,
Toward a path of feeling guided to that,
Irrelevant questions of a sincere system,
A unique type of soul stays within them,
An authentic life moves with free will,
No one knows the heights of the material,
Hold this eternal glimpse for a certain kind,
Incarnate into what is now in the mind,
A benevolent dissolve of lasting intuition,
Words used for another level of perception.

Basic & Integrated

The center core is always much more,
Selected circuit path to magnetically store,
Theories practiced within awareness,
The present moment aligns within this,
Dramatic mathematics to form language,
Interacting with one's innate courage,
To explain the complexity of the brain,
The unknown taken for granted as plain,
A needed formula of expressed variables,
Digital hardware, frequencies, & cables,
The connection is basic & integrated,
Receptive to a reflection now animated,
Biologically & naturally shown,
All of this is owned & known.

Compassion for Denial

I need to stand my ground & deny,
Yet I want you to please understand why,
It's a fragile balance of what I know,
For the understanding I hope to show,
Compassion for what I need to tell,
To look out for myself & others as well,
So many of the world's problems,
No one person can solve all of them,
It's humbling to know I can't help,
Particular areas in life where I fell,
Take what I say as an act of faith,
Just believe you will make your way,
I trust you can plan ahead,
To discern everything I just said.

An Unfolding Verse

Stillness within this settling view,
Visioning the next important thing to do,
This is for everyone to decide,
With life's movement, no one can hide,
It is life, for better or worse,
For myself, it is an unfolding verse,
I can wait; I can contemplate,
I could discuss the uncertainty of faith,
Yet, now I'll experience my senses,
Doubt in circumstance may prevent this,
Could I confess the fear I'm thinking about?
Merely a thought of worry or doubt,
As much as it may seem real,
It will pass & it is only how I feel.

What I've Done

What does it mean to be wrong?
A judgment of what I've done all along,
The best I knew how to do,
Yet different to what I now go through,
At times doing what I think I should,
Following true desire is just as good,
The blind fold is on my eyes,
Only until I know and realize,
The reality of letting God & letting go,
God can't make the decision for me, I know,
So I look for an insight to a better way,
To know what to think, feel, act on, or say,
I think there is timing for this to happen,
I'll escape the doubt I may be trapped in.

A Precious Girl

The breath is a wonderful thing,
Given & taken; the life that it can bring,
Inhaling in, the observed & learned,
Exhaling out, some writing to be discerned,
Unknown reason, pressure in circumstance,
Caught in worry, doubt, & a form of trance,
There is always time to let this go,
Being led to follow my heart & soul,
The other side of the equation is unknown,
Lack of focus, when what I offer is shown,
A design of the mind, wishing for a balance,
Admitting this attempt to make some sense,
An experience with thoughts of this world,
It is an eternal connection & a precious girl.

Extreme Thinking

A direction to approach in some way,
I'll draw conclusions on a situation today,
Although I may never know the truth of it,
What I do believe, is at the heart of it,
Lack of trust in this world & others,
For what I do, who I am, & all it covers,
Confidentially of myself & my Creator,
Secrets kept to respect & honor her,
Is there a risk by trusting this unknown?
A chance of emotional hurt may occur,
God's business, people's lives, & my own,
Where are the boundaries of respect shown?
Time & money; choice & consequence,
This cause & affect makes no sense.

Book on a Shelf

What is known & what is unknown?
To apply it to the current moment shown,
These feelings are based on thought,
A thought based story, the media bought,
Should I adopt this as what's real?
Its all good until my sins are revealed,
As a flawed & perfect man, in between,
Laws of nature & the mind will be seen,
Muddy water settles; chaotic mind clears,
Natural alignment to a wellbeing now here,
For gratitude based on its own self,
Consistent determination; a book on a shelf,
An organized possession, just living life,
Possibly he will find his beloved wife.

My Options

Once again, thinking of what to do,
My options as the day moves through,
Collected info for a knowledgeable stance,
I don't know what to do to break this trance,
So I'll think less to be who I am,
Letting pity pass by, for true faith to begin,
Am I looking for a search to believe?
If so, for what, when perception can deceive,
My lost capability to encourage & be kind,
Within an understanding in the mind,
Selection of seven billion people to give to,
Yet a day to day life to live through,
While a mental illness verges to heal me,
God & the devil, play games for all to see.

Mixed Interactions

We all have ideas about what we want,
Many views; the side, the back, & the front,
Faith within intuitive guidance to navigate,
A blissful epiphany opens my eyes & I wait,
Anything can happen in the present moment,
How is giving it away a form of owning it?
This situation is a gift to meditate on,
Acknowledging in life how far I've come,
Forgive me for trying to not judge you,
There must be a lot you're going through,
Or maybe it's just who you are,
I can't understand this from afar,
Wrapped up in dramatic simplicity,
All I need to do is just be me.

Index of Poems

About the Author

Daniel Feindt currently lives in Bucks County PA, where he has written many poems and self-published various books. Currently, Daniel also enjoys painting artwork with acrylics and works with web-design to share his work online.

In 1999, Daniel was diagnosed with schizophrenia. This is not seen as a negative label, but rather an expression within himself as a creative person. In an effort to understand the world he lives in, he has studied the nature of thought & the mind. Overall, his view is seen with gratitude.

Daniel's current philosophy on life is a balanced approach. This is shown not only in the writing of poetry, but in his artwork as well. An abstract ingredient is usually added to his expressions, to show the unknown patterns of life.

Printed in the United States
By Bookmasters